WRITING SOLUTIONS:

Beginnings,
Middles,
& Endings

COMMUNICATION TEXTBOOK SERIES
Jennings Bryant—Editor

Journalism
Maxwell McCombs—Advisor

BERNER • Writing Literary Features

FENSCH • The Sports Writing Handbook

TITCHENER • Reviewing the Arts

FENSCH • Writing Solutions: Beginnings, Middles, & Endings

WRITING SOLUTIONS

Beginnings,
Middles,
& Endings

Thomas Fensch
University of Texas at Austin

LEA **LAWRENCE ERLBAUM ASSOCIATES, PUBLISHERS**
1989 Hillsdale, New Jersey   Hove and London

Lawrence Erlbaum Associates, Inc., Publishers
365 Broadway
Hillsdale, New Jersey 07642

Production, interior, and
cover design: Robin Marks Weisberg

Library of Congress Cataloging in Publication Data

Fensch, Thomas.
    Writing solutions : beginnings, middles & endings / Thomas Fensch.
        p.   cm. — (Communication textbook series. Journalism)
    Bibliography: p.
    Includes index.
    ISBN 0-8058-0410-2.   ISBN 0-8058-0411-0 (pbk.)
    1. Journalism—Authorship.   I. Title.   II. Series.
PN4775.F38   1988
    808 ′.06607--dc19   88-13102
                                                                          CIP

Printed in the United States of America
10   9   8   7   6   5   4   3   2   1

For my friend and colleague
Gale Wiley
who has always believed in this book

Contents

_____ **2**

MIDDLES: MOVING THROUGH THE ARTICLE   73

_____ **3**

14 TYPES OF ENDINGS   112

Preface

"Writing is easy," Gene Fowler once said, *"all you have to do is sit staring at a blank sheet of paper until the drops of blood form on your forehead."*

It doesn't have to be *that hard.*

Whether you are a novice or intermediate Journalism student; in a freshman English class; writing a speech, a technical report, advertising copy, or promotional or publicity material; beginning a magazine article or a book; or working on any other writing project, you need to face the demands of that first blank page or that blank word processor screen. You need to not only fill that first page or screen; you need to begin your project effectively, introducing your subject to your reader with exactly the right beginning, and with confidence that you are expressing the right tone and style.

Writing Solutions fills a universal gap—this is a "generic" style book, if you will. It is deliberately not focused on journalism styles, nor focused for English 101 students, but is a style guide that can be used for all types of writing. It is also structured to be a self-help guide for writers who may not be enrolled in a college or university class. It also is not too advanced for high school writing projects.

This book is the result of my 20-year concentration in publishing nonfiction: newspaper articles, magazine articles, and books; and of my nearly 15 years of teaching writing techniques at the university level. It is designed to be as universally applicable as possible. Although most journalism books discuss specific journalism techniques, and a few "freshman English 101" style books discuss a few notable beginnings in contemporary literature, there has never been a book that shows a wide variety of beginnings that would be appropriate in most circumstances. This book fills that gap.

Stated simply, the more you know of technique, the easier everything becomes. The more styles of *beginnings* you know, the easier it is to conquer that blank page in your typewriter or move that blinking cursor across your blank computer screen.

The more *structure* (middles) you know, the easier it is to use the right form and to move through your work.

Choosing the right *ending* means the difference between letting your material "dribble off the last page" or ending with real emphasis and impact.

At about the same time Gene Fowler was sweating blood, sportswriter W. W. "Red" Smith said, "there's nothing to writing. All you do is sit down at the typewriter and open a vein."

Put away that knife and turn the page. Once you conquer beginnings, middles (structures or form), and endings, you won't have to sweat blood.

Or even open a vein.

Thomas Fensch

Acknowledgments

The author is grateful to the following individuals and firms which have granted rights to print or reprint copyrighted material:

Ackerman, Diana, material reprinted with permission;

The Associated Press, material reprinted with permission;

Atheneum Publishers, Charles S. Holmes, excerpted from *The Clocks of Columbus: The Literary Career of James Thurber.* Copyright © 1972 Charles S. Holmes. Reprinted with the permission of Atheneum Publishers, an imprint of Macmillan Publishing Company;

Austin American-Statesman, material reprinted with permission;

Better Homes & Gardens magazine, "Fever: New Facts You Should Know" and "Historic House Update: Is the National Register for You?" reprinted from *Better Homes and Gardens* magazine. Copyright Meredith Corporation 1986. All rights reserved;

Car & Driver magazine, material reprinted with permission;

Chicago Tribune wire service, material reprinted with permission of *The Chicago Tribune*;

Cottier, Montgomery, material reprinted with permission;

The Daily Texan, The University of Texas at Austin, material reprinted with permission of Texas Student Publications, Inc.;

The Dallas Times Herald, material reprinted with permission;

Evans, Jack, material reprinted with permission;

Fensch, Thomas, material reprinted with permission;

The Fort Worth Star Telegram, material reprinted with permission;

Fortune magazine, material reprinted with permission;

Harper & Row, Darwin Payne, *The Man of Only Yesterday: Frederick Lewis Allen,* copyright © 1975, reprinted with permission of Harper & Row;

Harvard Magazine, "Vita: Johann Mattheson, Versatile Musician" by Walter Schenkman, Sept.-Oct. issue, 1981. Copyright © 1981 *Harvard Magazine.* Reprinted by permission;

I.H.T. Corporation, Material by Red Smith reprinted with permission;

Kellman, Martin, material reprinted by permission of the author and *The Chronicle of Higher Education*;

Keteyian, Armen, material reprinted with permission;

King, Dr. Martin Luther Jr., material from "I have a dream" reprinted with permission of Joan Daves. Copyright © 1963 by Martin Luther King, Jr.;

KNT News Service, material reprinted with permission;

Little, Brown, Inc., material from *Walter Lippman and the American Century* by Ronald Steele. Copyright © 1980 by Ronald Steel reprinted by permission of Little, Brown and Company;

The Los Angeles Times, "Cattle Drive is Long, Hard—Right Out of Old West" by Ronald B. Taylor, published Oct. 13, 1986 and "Stricken With MS, Madlyn Rhue Still A Working Actress" by Howard Rosenberg, copyright 1986, 1987, *Los Angeles Times.* Reprinted by permission;

Macmillan, Inc., reprinted with permission of The Free Press, a Division of Macmillan, Inc. from *The Four Days of Courage: The Untold Story of the People Who Brought Marcos Down* by Bryan Johnson. Copyright © 1987 by Bryan Johnson;

The New York Times, "Pugilist's Progress" by David Kelly. Copyright © 1987 by The New York Times Company. Reprinted by permission. "Adultery with Discussions" by Wendy Lesser. Copyright © 1985 by The New York Times Company. Reprinted by permission. "Chopping down a forest of bad guys" by David Wiltse. Copyright © 1986 by The New York Times Company. Reprinted by permission. "Novelist in a Mirrow" by Richard Gilman. Copyright © 1986 by The New York Times Company. Reprinted by permission. "Atomic Bombing of Nagasaki Told By Flight Member" by William L. Lawrence. Copyright © 1945 by The New York Times Company. Reprinted by permission. "Open Road Beckons to Adventurer, Age 5" by Mark A. Uhlig. Copyright © 1987 by The New York Times Company. Reprinted by permission. "Sojourns in the Snow; Hitting the Heights at Jackson Hole" by Clifford D. May. Copyright © 1986 by The New York Times Company. Reprinted by permission;

Newsday, the article "Harrison Ford: Lucky, and Patient, Star" by Mike McGrady, copyright 1986, Newsday, Inc. Reprinted by permission;

Newsweek, material from the article "Small Screen's Big Credits" by Harry F. Waters, from *Newsweek,* Oct. 14, 1985, reprinted with permission;

The Philadelphia Inquirer, "When .10¢ equals $46,806, the IRS taxes a firm's patience" reprinted with permission from *The Philadelphia Inquirer,* 1986;

Prentice-Hall, Inc., William Metz, NEWSWRITING: From Lead to "30", 2/e, © 1985, p. 71. Reprinted by permission of Prentice-Hall, Inc., Englewood Cliffs, New Jersey;

Oxford University Press, from *Inside the Vicious Heart; Americans and the Liberation of Nazi Concentration Camps* by Robert H. Abzug. Copyright © 1985 by Robert H. Abzug. Reprinted by permission of Oxford University Press, Inc.;

Random House, material from *The Random House Handbook* by Frederick Crews, copyright © 1980 Random House, Inc., reprinted with permission of Random House, Inc.;

Schleuse, Doris Laird, material reprinted with permission;

Sport magazine, material reprinted with permission;

Sports Illustrated, the following article is reprinted courtesy of *Sports Illustrated* from the January 19, 1987 issue. Copyright © 1987, Time, Inc. "I Have Got to Do Right" by William Nack. All rights reserved;

The St. Louis Post-Dispatch, material reprinted with permission;

St. Martin's Press, material from *The Doctor and the Damned* by Albert Haas, copyright © 1984 St. Martin's Press, Inc., New York, reprinted with permission;

Time, excerpts from "How Reagan Stays Out of Touch" (December 8, 1986), "Hospitals Learn the Hard Sell" (January 12, 1987), "A Leader from the Last Days of Empire" (January 12, 1987), "Africa" (February 23, 1987) and "Magician of the Musical" (January 18, 1988), copyright © 1986, 1987, 1988, Time, Inc. All rights reserved. Reprinted by permission of Time, Inc.;

University of Chicago Press, first paragraph and last 4 paragraphs from "A River Runs Through It," from Maclean, Norman, *A River Runs Through It And Other Stories,* © 1976 by the University of Chicago Press. All rights reserved;

The Viking Press, from CANNERY ROW by John Steinbeck. Copyright 1945 by John Steinbeck. Copyright renewed © 1973 by The Estate of John Steinbeck. All rights reserved. Reprinted by permission of Viking Penguin Inc. From THE LOG FROM THE SEA OF CORTEZ by John Steinbeck. Copyright 1951 by John Steinbeck. Copyright renewed © 1979 by The Estate of John Steinbeck. All rights reserved. Reprinted by permission of Viking Penguin Inc. From OF MICE AND MEN by John Steinbeck. Copyright 1937, renewed © 1965 by John Steinbeck. All rights reserved. Reprinted by permission of Viking Penguin Inc.;

The Wall Street Journal, "Landlubber Reporter Sails the Atlantic and Survives, But Barely" by Paul B. Carroll. Reprinted by permission of *The Wall Street Journal,* © Dow Jones & Co., 1987. All rights reserved. "L.A. Law" by Martha Bayles. Reprinted by permission of *The Wall Street Journal,* © Dow Jones & Co., 1986. All rights reserved. "What Stops Hearts, Is Somewhat Sadistic and is 100 Years Old? by Cynthia Sanz. Reprinted by permission of *The Wall Street Journal,* © Dow Jones & Co., 1984. All rights reserved. "New Question in Race: Is Oldest President Showing His Age?" by James M. Perry and Rick Jaroslovsky. Reprinted by permission of *The Wall Street Journal,* © Dow Jones & Co., 1984. All rights reserved. "Struggling Back" by Jacob M. Schlesinger and Melinda Grenier Guiles. Reprinted by permission of *The Wall Street Journal,* © Dow Jones & Co., 1987. All rights reserved;

The Washington Post, material reprinted with permission;

Wysocki, Annette McGivney, material reprinted with permission;

Yankee magazine, material reprinted with permission.

To begin at the beginning is, next to ending at the end,
the whole art of writing.
—Hilaire Belloc

1

Beginnings:
What They Are, What They Do

> The White Rabbit put on his spectacles. "Where shall I begin, please your Majesty?" he asked.
> "Begin at the beginning," the King said, very gravely, "and go on till you come to the end: then stop."
> —*Alice's Adventures in Wonderland*

Whether you call it "The Narrative Hook," as many English professors do, or whether you call it "the Lead" (pronounced *leed*) as all journalists do, or whether you simply call it "The Beginning," (as we do throughout this book), the opening is crucial to your writing.

The beginning must be appropriate—and it is often the most difficult part of any writing project.

There are as many reasons for this difficulty as there are writers: Many approach their typewriters or word processors without a clear idea of what they want to write—or how they want to write it. Others begin page 1 with a clear idea of what they want to say, but without the experience to know exactly how to begin. Others know *approximately* what they want to say and *generally* how they want to write it, but lack the courage to begin. Because of these inabilities, some never begin page 1 at all.

In novice writers, this is sometimes called a *developmental* writer's block. Veteran writers develop writer's block for complex psychological reasons.

I have often felt that writer's block can be more easily conquered *with better knowledge of beginning techniques.* The novelist and nonfiction writer Isaac Asimov has said that he seldom—if ever—suffers from writer's block, and with good reason. With hundreds of published articles and over 400 pub-

1

lished books, he sits down to write entirely comfortable with his material and experienced enough to realize how to begin.

For most of the rest of us, without 400 published books, the writing is still hard. And the most difficult is the empty first page or the blank computer screen.

So how do you begin any writing project effectively—and appropriately? There are three key areas:

- Knowledge of your own abilities and experiences as a writer;
- Expectations of your audience—the publication you have in mind for your material and the expectations the readers have of that publication;
- And the demands of the subject you are writing about.

Any writer is better equipped to begin *any* project if he or she has a comprehensive command of possible beginnings. Those possible openings, combined with the expectations of your audience, plus the demands of the topic help target you toward the perfect lead.

If you miss that perfect lead for your material, you cannot hope a reader will jump from the beginning of your material and try again to read through the material from the middle on.

If you lose the reader with an inappropriate beginning, you have lost the reader forever.

What does the elusive perfect beginning do? What do you do, as a writer, when you begin on page 1?

The beginning should contain one (or both) of these Es and the I:

- It should *Entertain.* The beginning should pull the reader into the story (this is the "narrative hook" the English professors refer to). It should capture the reader's attention and not let the reader slip away at the beginning of the narrative;
- It should *Educate* the reader about the topic, whether the subject is medical or educational, national or local, specialized or general;
- It should *Involve* the reader in the story.

Additionally, it should capsulize or conceptualize the story for the reader in the first few paragraphs.

Equally important, the beginning *sets the tone of the complete story and the expertise or authority of the writer.* It is the author's firm handshake on meeting.

In almost all cases, the writing should be conversational in nature, as if the writer is talking to a close friend, telling a story face to face. For that is exactly what the writer *is* doing—telling a story to the reader. And thus, the writing style should be conversational, neither too formal nor too informal.

How long should a beginning be? There are some rules for some beginnings and no rules for others. Throughout this book, we offer the *suggested length* of each type of beginning. Additionally, when appropriate we offer an *Advisory,* a warning about any inappropriate uses of various beginnings, or tips about their use.

Because some beginnings are used daily, some often but not daily, and some used only occasionally, we offer guidelines regarding this usage. And we offer, on a numerical scale of 1-10, the *general* difficulty range of each beginning or lead.

In general, the beginnings are presented in order of difficulty from the easiest at the beginning, to the more complex; the most familiar at the beginning to the less familiar; the elemental to the most complex.

In this book, we make no distinction between beginnings for newspaper articles, magazine articles, or books, because there is no difference. To paraphrase Gertrude Stein, *a beginning is a beginning is a beginning.* Novelists and nonfiction authors have the same problems and the same aims when beginning their work as newspaper and magazine writers do: to capture their readers and not let them escape. Some novels—*Moby Dick, 1984,* and *A Tale of Two Cities,* to name just three—are memorable for their beginnings. To emphasize the Gertrude Stein paraphrase, we cite memorable book openings—and closings—throughout the book, in addition to memorable newspaper and magazine beginnings.

One final word: *No matter what type of beginning you use, it should come to an obvious conclusion.*

THE NEWSPAPER (TELEVISION & RADIO) NEWS LEAD

"President Reagan's new budget"

Ever since the Civil War, daily journalism in America has depended on a beginning that is usually called the *summary lead.* This is a beginning in which a news event—usually crime, accidents, fires, airplane or automobile accidents involving fatalities—is presented in summary form.

There is a simple key to writing this beginning: The writer asks, mentally:

- What happened?
- Where?
- When?

Using a specific day: Monday, Thursday, Saturday, and so on, rather than yesterday, today, tomorrow. An accident may occur on a Monday, but a daily newspaper may not be able to print the story until the next day's edition. Thus, if the reporter writes "Monday" and the reader reads the story on Tuesday, the reader will understand when the accident took place. If the writer inadvertently writes *today* (on Monday) and the reader reads the story on Tuesday, the reader assumes the "today" is Tuesday. In the world of daily journalism, whether you write for the *Morning Sun* or the *Evening Moon, The Daily Bugle,* or the daily whatever, readers will understand on Tuesday that an accident happened on Monday, if you write *Monday*.

If you answer the questions of: What happened, where, and when, in no more than three sentences *without using the victims' names,* that is the first paragraph.

The second paragraph should contain specific names in this descending order:

- Fatalities;
- Injuries;
- Property damage.

If there are no fatalities, then this order should be used:

- Injuries;
- Property damage next.

If there are no fatalities and no injuries, then property damage should be at the top of the second paragraph.

The third paragraph should contain the *most important fact or facts in the story.*

After some experience, daily newspaper reporters are able to write these *summary leads,* as they are called in journalism, as quickly as they are able to write.

This form is as appropriate for national journalism stories as it is for regional and local stories. Here is an example of such a story from *The Dallas Morning News* by reporter Jennifer Dixon (1987), using a *dateline* (the city where the story originated) at the beginning of the first line. (Pharr, Texas is at the southern tip of Texas, near the Mexican border and the Gulf of Mexico.)

> PHARR, Texas—A federal agent was gunned down on a dusty parking lot just north of the Mexican border when a drug arrest exploded into gunfire, officials said Thursday.
>
> Drug Enforcement Administration Special Agent William Ramos, 30, was shot in the chest Wednesday while trying to arrest a narcotics suspect on new Year's Eve, said Ken Miley, DEA agent in charge of the McAllen district office.

Felipe Molina-Uribe, 29, a McAllen man who suffered a leg wound in the shoot-out, was arrested at the scene and charged with killing a federal agent, Assistant U.S. Attorney Christopher Milner said. He was under guard at an area hospital.

Variation.   If the story does not involve accidents with fatalities or injuries, but does involve "big numbers" federal, state, or local tax dollars or other major funding, the *largest numbers* go to the top of the story. This is an Associated Press wire service lead from Washington, "moved" (sent) on the AP news system the first week in 1987:

WASHINGTON (AP)—The Education Department will ask Congress next week to earmark 600 million of its new budget for an innovative loan program that would let students borrow up to $50,000 and peg repayments to their incomes.

The "Income Contingent Loan" program—the loans would be called ICL—will be included in the Reagan administration spending plan to be submitted Monday to Congress.

"We believe this is the single biggest advance in the financing of higher education for students in the last 15 years," deputy education undersecretary Bruce Carnes said.

Using this lead, a newspaper writer uses *the most important facts first* in the story and continues to write the story from the most important facts at the top of the story to the least important facts at the bottom of the story.

Second Variation.   If there are no fatalities or no injuries in the story, but if the story is about a major national, regional, or local figure, then the reporter may place the name of the official first, *if the name of the personality is more important than any other fact in the story.*

Here is how the beginning of such an article might be written:

WASHINGTON—President Reagan's schedule for the coming weekend is a light one, the White House press office announced Tuesday.

Late Friday he will travel by helicopter to Camp David, where he will videotape a five-minute national appeal for the United Way. He will also meet with representatives from Chile and meet with national Boy Scout leaders. He will return to the White House late Sunday afternoon.

Name: Newspaper News lead.

Frequency of use: Daily, in all major newspapers in the country.

Length: Three paragraphs, with a maximum of three sentences in each paragraph.

Difficulty Range: 1–3. Easy with practice.

Advisory.   This lead is also appropriate for radio and television news reporters, but because of problems involving how listeners assimilate radio and TV news, these leads for radio and TV *should be no more than three sentences long,* not three paragraphs long.

THE STATEMENT BEGINNING

"Elmer Gantry was drunk. He was eloquently drunk"

This opening could be called the *status* or *situation* beginning because it states the status or situation of a subject at the beginning of the article, in plain declarative sentences. This technique may not appear to be "literary" or sophisticated, but many stories demand such a beginning. This beginning is especially appropriate when writing about national subjects, or medicine or finance or any other topic that may change over a period of time. It is also an appropriate beginning when a simple anecdote about an individual may not tell the whole story.

Here is the deceptively simple beginning to Truman Capote's classic *In Cold Blood:*

> The village of Holcomb stands on the high wheat plains of western Kansas, a lonesome area that other Kansans call 'out there.' "

And here is the statement beginning to Sinclair Lewis's *Elmer Gantry:*

> Elmer Gantry was drunk. He was eloquently drunk, lovingly and pugnaciously drunk.

And the statement beginning from Margaret Mitchell's *Gone With the Wind:*

> Scarlet O'Hara was not beautiful, but men seldom realized it when caught by her charm. . . .

Many statement beginnings are longer and more detailed than a simple paragraph.

Here, from *Fortune* magazine, is the cover story, by Roy Rowan (1986), a story the *Fortune* editors titled "The 50 Biggest Mafia Bosses." The subtitle was: "Meet the men who manage a $50-billion-a-year business that reaches into almost every U.S. city. They face familiar problems: aging leadership, less dedicated younger employees, increased foreign competition. And now the feds are trying to wreck their profit centers."

> Crime pays. Annual gross income from the rackets will probably exceed $50 billion this year. That makes the mob's business greater than all U.S. iron, steel,

copper, and aluminum manufacturing combined, or about 1.1% of the GNP. These figures, compiled for the President's Commission on Organized Crime, include only revenues from traditional mob businesses, such as narcotics, loan-sharking, illegal gambling, and prostitution. They do not include billions more brought in from the mob's diversification into such legitimate enterprises as entertainment, construction, trucking, and food and liquor wholesaling.

The industry that runs this huge part of the economy comprises crime families, not companies. Wharton Econometric Forecasting Associates, in a study prepared for the President's Crime Commission, found that the mob's hold on the economy stifles competition and siphons off capital, resulting in a loss of some 400,000 jobs, an increase in consumer prices of 0.3%, a reduction in total output of $18 billion, and a decrease in per capita disposable income of $77 a year. Since organized-crime members cheat on taxes, the rest of the population will pay an estimated $6.5 billion more to the Internal Revenue Service this year. (p. 24)

Although this opening may appear intimidating, the first paragraph contains only five sentences, the second paragraph three.

Many statement openings are not even that "massive." Here is a statement lead from an article "When 10¢ Equals $46,806, The IRS Taxes A Firm's Patience." This article, by reporter Arthur W. Howe (1986), which appeared in *The Philadelphia Inquirer,* won the Roy W. Howard Award in the 1986 Scripps Howard Foundation National Journalism Awards.

It began with a dispute over a dime.

The Internal Revenue Service contended that Rohm & Haas Co. owed it $4,488,112.98 in payroll taxes for the period that ended June 30, 1983. The giant chemical manufacturer had deposited $4,488,112.88—exactly 10 cents less.

One month later, Rohm & Haas received a notice from the IRS's Philadelphia service center. The agency sought a penalty for the 10-cent late payment.

The penalty: $46,806.37.

"Try and figure that one out. How do you explain it? It was so unbelievable," said Thomas C. Friel, manager of corporate taxes for Rohm & Haas.

Rohm & Haas is not alone. Representatives of a number of Philadelphia area corporations, large and small, say that dealing with the regional office of the IRS can be a nightmarish experience.

Executives say that over the years they have received dozens—in some cases, hundreds—of erroneous notices from the IRS service center computer.

They also say that correspondence with the service center is rarely acknowledged, that minor tax problems can take months—or years to resolve, that the agency's computer and employees routinely make mathematical errors of epic proportions, and that tax deposits can disappear as mysteriously as they can suddenly reappear in a company's bank account.

Finally, another statement opening, by Denis Collins (1987), from a story moved by the Knight-Ridder News Service in January:

SAN JOSE, Calif.—As hunting dogs go, Robert Outman's beagles are high-priced and well-protected. Each of his 50 dogs is insured for $25,000 by Lloyd's of London. And their work is backed by a million-dollar guarantee.

For all that, you might reasonably expect the dogs' quarry to be worthy of a Remington painting—snarling beasts, sharp of fang and claw. But Outman's beagles hunt less ferocious prey. The trail they follow, along the baseboards of suburbia, lead to termites.

"People are still skeptical, but we have passed the test of time," said Outman, who in 1979 founded TADD Services Corp. in Belmont. The initials stand for Termite and Ant Detection Dogs. And the services they perform, seeking out wood-eating pests where human inspectors cannot go, has provided both national attention and controversy. Home sellers and the more conventional pest-control companies are understandably hostile to the idea.

"I guess you could say I have a rather negative opinion of it," said Marv Klingenberg, the San Jose manager of Orkin Exterminating, the largest pest-control company in the nation. "But it is a novel idea."

Name: Statement opening.

Frequency of use: Often seen in books, newspapers, and magazines.

Length: Varies with subject, usually three to six paragraphs.

Difficulty range: 2–4. Usually relatively easy to construct.

THE DESCRIPTIVE BEGINNING

"The Salinas River drops in close to the hillside"

In this opening, the writer paints a word picture of the subject. This picture may be brief—or extensive and highly detailed, but it is a visual image—constructed so the reader can see the subject or the portrait in the mind's eye.

Here, by Bill James (1986), published in *Sport* magazine, is a portrait beginning of an article about Casey Stengel:

> It will be several years yet until those of us who did not know Casey Stengel personally are allowed to have any opinions about him. From among the gallery of remembered titans who populated New York hardball in the Fifties, from the moments spent with Joe and Jackie and Willie and Mickey and Billy and Whitey and the Duke and Yogi, this now aging generation of sportswriters treasures most the remembered moments spent with a cantankerous, theatrical, lumpy, ancient, nervous, tough, clowning, spitting, awkward, shuffling, dissembling, old coot resembling nothing so much as a wax bust of a not particularly attractive Roman emperor that had been set too near a fire. (p. 85)

Note that the descriptive lead does not necessarily have to be a "litany of adjectives" that James uses: cantankerous, theatrical, lumpy, ancient—

and the rest, but the description *does* have to be striking. His chain of adjectives coupled with that marvelous phrase "resembling nothing so much as a wax bust of a not particularly attractive Roman emperor that had been set too near a fire" certainly captures Stengel to me.

But the descriptive opening is not necessarily limited to personality portraits. Here is John Steinbeck's beginning to his novel *Of Mice and Men:*

> A few miles south of Soledad, the Salinas River drops in close to the hillside bank and runs deep and green. The water is warm too, for it has slipped twinkling over the yellow sands in the sunlight before reaching the narrow pool. On one side of the river the golden foothill slopes curve up to the strong and rocky Gabilan mountains, but on the valley side the water is lined with trees—willows fresh and green with every spring, carrying in their lower leaf junctures the debris of the winter's flooding; and sycamores with mottled, white, recumbent limbs and branches that arch over the pool. On the sandy bank under the trees the leaves lie deep and so crisp that a lizard makes a great skittering if he runs among them. Rabbits come out of the brush to sit on the sand in the evening, and the damp flats are covered with the night tracks of 'coons, and with the spread pads of dogs from the ranches, and with the split-wedge tracks of deer that come to drink in the dark.
>
> There is a path through the willows and among the sycamores, a path beaten hard by boys coming down from the ranches to swim in the deep pool, and beaten hard by tramps who come wearily down from the highway in the evening to jungle-up near water. In front of the low horizontal limb of a giant sycamore there is an ash pile made by many fires; the limb is worn smooth by men who have sat on it. (p. 7)

Look again at Steinbeck's adjectives and phrases: *slipped twinkling over the yellow sands, the golden foothill slopes, willows fresh and green with every spring, sycamores with mottled, white, recumbent limbs;* his notice of the *'coon* tracks (not the more formal *racoon* tracks) and dog tracks and deer tracks, the path beaten hard by the boys coming to swim and beaten hard by the tramps who *come wearily* to *jungle-up* near water; the ash pile from *many fires* and the *limb worn smooth* from those who have sat on it.

The descriptive opening is often necessary to *set the scene* for the reader. To succeed in this, the writer must visit the scene enough to be able to recall it later—taking notes with a note pad is a must, but there are at least two variations on notetaking: The reporter may use a portable tape recorder to make a tape record of the scene—the tape may be kept and replayed as the reporter writes the story.

The reporter may also use a Polaroid or other "instant" camera to take snapshots to use later as a reminder of what the scene looked like. These can be propped beside the typewriter or word processor as memory aids as the reporter begins the story.

We all carry "snapshots" in our imagination of what certain scenes look like—we all have "stylized" or "cliche" portraits in our memory of what

Niagara Falls looks like—or what Old Faithful looks like, or the Eiffel Tower. If the reporter is writing about a scene that is not as universally known as Niagara Falls, then it is the reporter's job to write the scene so strikingly that the reader can visualize it, either as a half-melted emperor's wax bust in the case of the Casey Stengel description on the well-wrought picture of the Salinas River, in Steinbeck's *Of Mice and Men.*

Name: Descriptive opening.

Frequency of use: Often seen.

Length: Varies with subject.

Difficulty range: 3–6. The writer must take notes, or use a tape recorder or camera to aid in describing the scene later as the story is written.

Advisory. *Do not assume that a photographer will tell your story for you.* If your material demands a descriptive opening, make sure the description *is in the story* not left to a photographer to picture. *A picture is not necessarily worth a thousand words* (especially if, for editing reasons, planned photos are not included in the final published "text-and-photos" story).

THE NARRATIVE ("ACTION") BEGINNING

"People Power reacted with courage"

This beginning could be called the *action* beginning or the *big play* beginning *because it shows something happening.* This beginning is related to the descriptive beginning because the writer still describes a scene to the reader, but in this beginning, there is motion, movement, action.

And this beginning can be simple or complex, according to the writer and to the event.

Here is the beginning of Bryan Johnson's (1987) book *The Four Days of Courage: The Untold Story of the People Who Brought Marcos Down.* Nothing could have more impact than his beginning. Notice, too, how he places himself in the action subtly, with the four words "the Filipinos around me." This action technique is just as effective for any other subject, for any other writing project, as it is in Johnson's book.

THEY RAN *TOWARDS* THE DANGER. When the crunch came, when that first column of Marine tanks smashed through a concrete wall and churned across a vacant field, the Filipinos around me hesitated for just a moment. "Jesus Christ!" yelled a kid in a blue T-shirt, heading instinctively for the machines, "they're trying to get around us!" The anonymous young man vaulted the six-foot wall and disappeared. Within second, two dozen others had followed. By the time all nine tanks had formed up for the attack, they were engulfed in a human sea.

People Power reacted with courage to its first sight of firepower, but it was a courage of trembling lips and of eyes brimming with tears. The thousands of nuns, housewives, school kids, ordinary people, and hard-core activists were brave enough to lay their bodies under the treads of tanks—but most were too terrified to look at them. They fixed their gaze on the scrubgrass, or cast imploring glances to the sky, while the stench of exhaust choked them and coated them with filth.

Why did the ground shake so violently? Was it the pulsating roar of the tanks, or was it all of us trembling together? People clasped hands instinctively and inched forward. Nuns clung to their rosaries, thrusting them heavenward, squeezing their eyes shut, reciting the Sorrowful Mysteries too fast for anyone to follow. And all the while, halted by the barricade of lying, sitting, kneeling people, the tanks continued to roar at full throttle.

It was an eternity, perhaps five minutes, before one tank hatch popped open with a metallic clank and a Marine looked out. Muffled radio messages could be heard from inside. More hatches opened, and other soldiers clambered out onto their machines in camouflage fatigues, encased in criss-crossed ammunition belts with bullets the size of fountain pens. These were combat soldiers, just arrived from the guerrilla war in Mindanao. They had a reputation as the country's toughest sons-of-bitches and now they played that role to the hilt. The crowd's chants of "Co-ry! Co-ry! Co-ry!" were met by stone faces or outright sneers. Those who pressed forward to offer cigarettes and flowers were dissuaded by Armalite assault rifles, pointed without waver towards the human barricade.

The Ferdinand Marcos forces in that first confrontation seemed uniformed clones of the President himself: deadly, ruthless, and utterly contemptuous of the average Filipino. They had rolled out of Fort Bonafacio like a conquering army on a routine mopping-up exercise—exuding haughty indifference as they squatted beside 50-caliber machine guns and dandled M-16s on their knees. And why not? The military split that Sunday afternoon was 200,000-to-500 in favor of Marcos. His loyal soldiers had nothing to fear from Juan Ponce Enrile and General Fidel Ramos, much less the unarmed rabble who supported them. (pp. 13–14)

This is also a perfect sports story beginning, if the writer can isolate one play that was crucial to a football game or baseball game or basketball game, or other sport.

In the following story of the Denver Bronco–Patriots game Sunday, Jan. 4, 1987, Knight-Ridder writer Jerry Greene (1987) begins with a "big play" lead—a quarterback "sack" for a safety late in the game:

DENVER—Defensive end Rulon Jones placed Denver in the AFC championship game by sacking New England quarterback Tony Eason for a safety that clinched the Broncos' 22–17 victory Sunday at Mile High Stadium.

Bronco fans—a record sellout of 76,105—were higher than their stadium when Jones sacked Eason with 1:37 remaining, ending New England's hopes of returning to the Super Bowl.

Denver (12–5) will travel to Cleveland (13–4) to play the Browns for the AFC title Sunday. It's a rare treat for the Broncos and their fans as Denver's last playoff victory was in 1977. They had lost four consecutive playoff games since then.

"I've been thinking for six years about how it would feel to win a playoff game," Denver Coach Dan Reeves said. "Now I can't describe the feeling because it's more than I ever imagined. The biggest feeling is pride for this team.

"And the biggest play was Rulon's sack. You have to count on your great players in games like this and Rulon came through when we had to have it."

The sack by Jones, who led the Broncos with a club-record 13½ sacks this season, climaxed an erratic but thrilling game in which the lead changed hands five times and neither team led by more than four until the end.

This six-paragraph beginning is appropriate for newspapers, yet the action beginning can be far, far longer, with just as much impact and just as much interest. Armen Keteyian (1982) used a long action beginning in his article, "How Julie Moss Found Ecstasy After Losing to Agony," which appeared in *The San Diego Union:*

All you could think was "Oh God, she's going to fall again. She's 15 feet from the finish line. 15 lousy feet from all the glory she deserves, and she's going to fall again. Dammit, she's not going to make it."

For nearly 12 hours, she had given everything the human spirit can ask of the human body. The race, this 140.6-mile torture test called the triathlon, had been hers since five miles into the marathon. She had passed the previous tests— the 2.4 mile swim in the Pacific, the 112-mile bike ride. Now, with 15 feet to go in the 26.2-mile run, her world was falling apart. The finish line was almost close enough to touch, but she looked as if she couldn't possibly get there.

Her legs, so rubbery they looked like jelly, shook and then surrendered.

She had fallen the first time 440 yards from the finish and sat there, dazed and staring at the street, unable to rise for nearly three minutes. Finally, she struggled to her feet and forged on.

With less than 100 yards left and her nearest competitor closing fast, she collapsed again. And got up. With less than 50 feet left, her legs gave way once more. Some race officials tried to help her to her feet so she could finish. Somehow she picked herself up again.

Now, for the fourth time, she was down— a frail, crumpled heap on the ground, 15 pathetic feet from a dream.

The streets of Kona, on the Big Island of Hawaii, had been packed with partiers—"It looked like the Rose Parade," she would say later—but they had fallen silent. No celebration now. The surrealistic side of sport had taken over. The revelers could do nothing more than bear witness. A courageous Raggedy Ann look-alike seemed to be struggling for her life at dusk.

This happened February 6. Thirteen days later, in living rooms across America, millions of people watching ABC's "Wide World of Sports" saw the tapes of this utterly compelling spectacle and sat stunned, collectively thinking the only possible thought: "If anything is fair in this world, let Julie Moss get up right now. Let her walk, stagger or crawl those last 15 feet. Let her finish. Let her be the women's winner in the World Ironman Championships. Please."

In the background, a haunting, beautiful instrumental tune played on.

Commentators Diana Nyad and Jim Lampley said nothing. Minutes earlier, after the second fall, Nyad had delicately explained a substance on Moss' shorts, saying, "In situations of extreme stress, you sometimes lose control over bodily functions."

There was nothing left to say now. It was only Moss and that mysterious music. All the crowd could do was hope.

"I couldn't see their faces," Moss said recently, drawing lines in the sand at Cardiff Beach near her home in Carlsbad as she thought back to the scenes that gripped a national television audience. "All I could feel was arms actually trying to lift me and carry me along. The energy was unbelievable.

"Then I looked up and saw Kathleen cross the finish line."

The race was over. Kathleen McCartney of Costa Mesa had won. Moss could have quit. Instead, she started to crawl. Slowly, agonizingly—red head down, one thin arm in front of the other—she crawled.

No one can describe the sight of such an athlete as this, beyond the limits of exhaustion, crawling to a finish line. Nobody tried. Only the music played on.

One minute later, the odyssey ended. Julie Moss wobbled and fell once more. When she did, her left hand felt the finish line. No matter that she was second. Incredibly, she had made it.

You wanted to cry. Many did.

"Have you ever seen pictures of dead people?" she says now, her freckled face very much alive. "When I saw the picture of the finish line, I thought: 'That's what dead people look like.' But you know what? My eyes were closed, but I was smiling. I knew, finally, it was all over."

No it wasn't. The story of 23-year-old Julie Moss, who grew up loving the beach in Carlsbad, was only beginning. From that moment Moss, even more than winner McCartney, became to many viewers an instant and authentic heroine, an unforgettable inspiration.

This beginning demands that the writer witness the sports event, take copious notes and—most importantly—recognize the crucial play when it occurs. If this is toward the end of the event—such as these two sports stories, the writer must describe the big play, then go back and summarize all the action that occurred before that crucial event.

Name: Narrative ("Action") Beginning.

Frequency of use: Often seen.

Difficulty range: 4–6. Reporter must be able to recognize the action or big play as significant when it occurs and write the story from that point first.

Advisory. Key beginning for many stories; especially appropriate for sports stories, in newspaper or magazine form.

THE ANECDOTE BEGINNING

"When they needed help, McCook was there"

This is a small true story on top of the larger, complete story.

Anecdotes are vignettes we know and treasure about people. They show character, motivation, behavior. They are the yardsticks by which we measure people.

Most anecdotes are probable (and verifiable); some historical anecdotes may be apocryphal. "I cannot tell a lie, Father, I cut down the cherry tree," George Washington said. True or not? We may never know, but we value that because it (presumably) shows Washington's character.

The anecdote beginning may be the single most effective technique for beginning a personality portrait or a profile.

Here is an ideal anecdotal beginning from a profile by Scot Meyer (1986), published in *The Austin American-Statesman*. The article was a profile of Prof. Jane McCook, who was retiring from the faculty of Southwestern University, in Georgetown, Texas, after a 32-year teaching career. The article was published under the title and subtitle:

Being there when
friends are in need

Former teacher says she 'just likes people'

Joyce Price Manford remembers attending a birthday party at her friend Jane McCook's house in 1975. Jane's father-in-law was celebrating his 80th birthday, and he had just blown out the candles on his cake.

That's when Manford slipped away, and went to lie down in the bedroom. She was having a heart attack.

"It wasn't two minutes until Jane missed me," Manford said recently. McCook saw that her friend was sick, and called a doctor who lived nearby.

"Jane directed everyone from her home with her telephone. After sending me (by ambulance) from the house, she called my family in Austin, then she talked back and forth from my husband's office in Austin and to the hospital in Georgetown. She kept everyone informed until I arrived at Seton (hospital). By her actions, she may well have saved my life—another example of the kind of friend she is."

Not all are quite so dramatic, but most of Jane McCook's friends have stories like that. Stories about how, when they needed help, McCook was there. The explanation, McCook said, is simple. "I've just always liked people." (Neighbor section, p. 1)

This beginning shows conflict, plunges the reader into the story, and shows the principal character in action.

The anecdote is *usually* positive in nature, and eventually proves a point.

During research for a published article, the writer should ask, "What's your own favorite story?" Or, the writer might ask friends "B," "C," or "D," "What is your favorite story about your friend "A"?

If the anecdote proves to be a favorite of the subject, it may well be the key to the story; an appropriate and ideal beginning.

Name: Anecdote beginning.

Frequency of use: Often seen.

Length: Varies with subject.

Difficulty range: 2–4. Usually easy to use.

Advisory. A practically perfect beginning for personality profiles.

THE MULTIPLE ANECDOTE BEGINNING

"Many hospitals are taking a few lessons"

This could be called the multiple anecdote or the multiple *example* beginning, because the writer offers a variety of evidence about a complex topic, or several aspects of a subject.

The writer offers these anecdotes or topics in a paragraph-by-paragraph or section-by-section form in the beginning of the article. *Time* staffer Stephen Koepp (1987) used such a beginning in an article titled "Hospitals Learn the Hard Sell," in an issue of *Time*. The article was subtitled "Feverish competition brings hype to the health care industry":

> The U.S. medical establishment may still draw its primary inspiration from the Hippocratic oath, but many hospitals are taking a few lessons from Madison Avenue. Items:
> • Mount Sinai Medical Center in Miami Beach is selling its own brand of chicken soup, complete with the hospital name on the label. Reason: to promote its reputation as a warm and soothing place.
> • SwedishAmerican Hospital in Rockford, Ill., is offering a clever gimmick to lure obstetrics customers: Dial-A-Dad, a service in which beepers are given to expectant fathers so they can be paged within a 30-mile radius when mothers go into labor.
> • "Kidney stones? Who ya Gotta Call . . . Stonebusters!" With that jarring punch line, Saint Joseph Medical Center in Burbank, Calif., is touting its newly acquired lithotriper, a device that disintegrates kidney stones with shock waves.
> What is this hype all about healing? Dr. Ben Casey, the stuffy TV neurosurgeon of yesteryear, would surely be stunned. While many doctors still keep a low advertising profile, the rest of the health-care industry has suddenly gone for the hard sell. To fill a growing number of empty beds and to stand

out amid increased competition, hospitals and clinics have started embracing modern marketing techniques. Result: a wave of come-ons from everything from cancer treatment to fat removal. (p. 56)

Here is another multiple example beginning by David Streitfield (1987), in an article about changing lifestyles. This article was published in *The Washington Post:*

Excess on the Rocks

The reckless become moderate as pleasures turns to dangers

Welcome to the Age of Moderation. The slogan: Down With Excess. The look: Simple. The motive: Survival.

Sex with a number of partners, smoking, drinking and consumption of high-cholesterol red meat all seem to be in decline. Even drug abuse, the spector of which was kindled into a national frenzy last year, is holding steady. Some evidence:

• The slide in apparent liquor consumption has been accelerating. Between 1975 and 1985, consumption fell 0.2 percent a year, according to the Distilled Spirits Council. From 1980 to 1985, it sank 2.4 percent. Nearly all the sales growth in wine over the last five years has come with the introduction of the less alcoholic wine coolers.

• The number of adult smokers dived from 37 percent of the population in 1975 to 30 percent last year, according to the American Cancer Sociey. Actual cigarette consumption slid 1.7 percent in 1986, the Department of Commerce says. This year the department projects another 2 percent drop. Smoking in public places is under attack from several quarters and has been greatly restricted by many municipalities, including Austin.

• Consumption of red meat—beef, pork, veal and lamb—declined from 147.7 pounds per capita in 1980 to 144.4 pounds in 1985, according to the Department of Agriculture.

• Contrary to public impression, illegal drug use has not been growing. Lucy Walker of the National Institute on Drug Abuse said, "From 1979 to '82, drug use went down a bit, and it's been stable from 1982 to 1985."

• Finally, in response to AIDS, polls are showing people as being more careful in their choice of sexual partners. For instance, a *Newsweek* survey in November said 58 percent of those polled or people they know are more cautious.

Why this trend toward temperance? With AIDS, it's self preservation. Are those other cutbacks equally a matter of choice?

"The more complicated the world becomes, the more important simplicity—including moderation—is. One of the recurring motives in the history of those Americans voluntarily opting for simpler living is to achieve greater independence, self-reliance and ultimately autonomy," said David Shi, professor of history at Davidson College in North Carolina and author of books on the simple life.

The reason? "If you rely overmuch on anything—from drugs, alcohol and tobacco to an addictive activity like compulsive shopping or a sedentary way of life—you not only run the risk of losing your independence, but of losing your life."

The writer may use a summary paragraph *before* the anecdotes or the summary material may be held until after the examples. To show that there are several separate topics, the writer may wish to use an asterisk or star or "bullet" or other typographic device to highlight the topics for the reader.

Name: Multiple example beginning.

Frequency of use: Often seen in complex subjects.

Length: Varies with topic.

Difficulty range: 3-5. Writers should pick significant anecdotes for the top of the story.

Advisory. To allow the beginning to be comprehensive, there should be three to seven topics. More than seven may drag the beginning to an overly complex length.

THE "I" BEGINNING

"Call me Ishmael"

In this beginning, the writer tells his story directly to the reader. This form is as old as ancient myths, when medicine men told folktales to tribes. Later adventurers told their stories, using the same beginning. One of the most famous "I" beginnings in classical literature is from Melville's *Moby Dick.* You may remember the beginning sentence. Do you know the entire first paragraph?

Call me Ishmael. Some years ago—never mind how long precisely—having little or no money in my purse, and nothing particular to interest me on shore, I thought I would sail about a little and see the watery part of the world. It is a way I have of driving off the spleen, and regulating the circulation. Whenever I find myself growing grim about the mouth; whenever it is a damp, drizzly November in my soul; whenever I find myself involuntarily pausing before coffin warehouses, and bringing up the rear of every funeral I meet; and especially whenever my hypos get such an upper hand of me, that it requires a strong moral principle to prevent me from deliberately stepping into the street, and methodically knocking people's hats off—then, I account it high time to get to sea as soon as I can. This is my substitute for pistol and ball. With a philosophical flourish Cato throws himself upon his sword; I quickly take to the ship. There is nothing surprising in this. If they but know it, almost all men in their degree, some time or other, cherish very nearly the same feelings towards the ocean with me.

In *Tough, Sweet & Stuffy: An Essay on Modern American Prose Styles,*
Walker Gibson (1966) wrote:

> The first-person-singular narrator telling his own story has a long and distin-
> guished history, and in some works of the past he has been clothed with enough
> complexity and self-consciousness to please almost anybody. (Sterne's Tristram
> Shandy is an example.) Simpler creations, in which a fictitious narrator-hero
> straightforwardly relates the story of his life, have produced some of literature's
> most venerable monuments. Once again, preparing to taste the full flavor of
> our own time, let us recall a narrating voice from the good gray nineteenth cen-
> tury. Here is David Copperfield introducing himself:
>   Whether I shall turn out to be the hero of my own life, or whether that sta-
> tion will be held by anybody else, these pages must show. To begin my life with
> the beginning of my life, I record that I was born (As I have been informed
> and believe) on a Friday, at twelve o'clock at night. It was remarked that the
> clock began to strike and I began to cry, simultaneously.
>   In consideration of the day and hour of my birth, it was declared by the
> nurse and by some sage women in the neighborhood who had taken a lively
> interest in me several months before there was any possibility of our becoming
> personally acquainted, first that I was destined to be unlucky in life; and secondly,
> that I was privileged to see ghosts and spirits: both these gifts inevitably at-
> taching, as they believed, to all unlucky infants of either gender born toward
> the small hours of the morning. (pp. 57–58)

Gibson also wrote:

> Now, with the familiar gentlemenly sounds of Mr. Copperfield ringing in the
> ear, let us try this introduction from another autobiography in fiction, com-
> posed just about a century later and rapidly becoming almost as familiar:
>   I am an American, Chicago-born—Chicago, that somber city—and go at
> things as I have taught myself, freestyle, and will make the record in my own
> way: first to knock, first admitted; sometimes an innocent knock, sometimes
> not so innocent. But a man's character is his fate, says Heraclitus, and in the
> end there isn't any way to disguise the nature of the knocks by acoustical work
> on the door or by gloving the knuckles.
>   Everybody knows there is no fineness or accuracy in suppression; if you hold
> down one thing you hold down the adjoining.
>   My own parents were not much to me, though I cared for my mother. She
> was simple-minded, and what I learned from her was not what she taught, but
> on the order of object lessons. She didn't have much to teach, poor woman.
> (pp. 58–59)

That's Augie March, in Saul Bellow's *The Adventures of Augie March.*
Gibson observed:

> The abrupt changes in tone may be bewildering, but they are spectacular. Wisdom
> from the Greeks is followed by the informality of "there isn't any way." The

polysyllables of "no fineness or accuracy in suppression" are followed by the conversational "if you hold down one thing, you hold down the adjoining." But does Augie know what he's doing? I am not sure. Does Bellow? . . .

But Augie, of course, is no idiot. As the rest of this huge novel makes plain, Augie is a bright, resourceful, thoughtful, poverty-stricken, opportunistic, self-educated young man raised on the seamy side of Chicago and it may be that this mixed background can make his mixed way of talk plausible. The hint of innocence we see in these opening lines continues in the book. (p. 61)

Here are two more "I" beginnings from books that have also become American classics:

If you really want to hear about it, the first thing you'll probably want to know is where I was born, and what my lousy childhood was like. . . .

My first recollection, Douglas MacArthur was fond of saying, "is that of a bugle call."

The first is J.D. Salinger's *The Catcher in the Rye* and the second is William Manchester's *American Caesar: Douglas MacArthur, 1880–1964*.

Although Herman Melville's Ishmael certainly sounds modern (the "damp, drizzly November in my soul . . ."), the "I" beginning often can be used much more dramatically. This is a perfect beginning for confessional material.

One of the most charming "I" form beginnings in recent literature is the slight variation of the "I"—the "we," in the opening paragraphs from Norman Maclean's *A River Runs Through It and Other Stories:*

In our family, there was no clear line between religion and fly fishing. We lived at the junction of great trout rivers in western Montana, and our father was a Presbyterian minister and a fly fisherman who tied his own flies and taught others. He told us about Christ's disciples being fishermen, and we were left to assume, as my brother and I did, that all first-class fishermen on the Sea of Galilee were fly fishermen and that John, the favorite, was a dry-fly fisherman. (p. 1)

We stated earlier that *a beginning is a beginning is a beginning*; it matters not whether that beginning might be for a newspaper or magazine article; a good beginning may be equally appropriate for fiction or for radio or television scriptwriting. Or for oratory.

On August 28, 1963, the Rev. Martin Luther King Jr. spoke on the steps of the Lincoln Memorial, in Washington, capping the March on Washington for Jobs and Freedom, in which 200,000 participated. Do you recall the theme of Dr. King's speech? Many do. It stands as his greatest public speech. And it reads like great literature, not "just" another Washington speech. Here is the end of Dr. King's speech. You remember it by the four-word title:

"I have a dream."

I say to you today, my friends, that in spite of the difficulties and frustrations of the moment I still have a dream. It is a dream deeply rooted in the American dream.

I have a dream that one day this nation will rise up and live out the true meaning of its creed: "we hold these truths to be self-evident; that all men are created equal."

I have a dream that one day on the red hills of Georgia the sons of former slaves and the sons of former slaveowners will be able to sit down together at the table of brotherhood.

I have a dream that one day even the state of Mississippi, a desert state sweltering with the heat of injustice and oppression, will be transformed into an oasis of freedom and justice.

I have a dream that my four little children will one day live in a nation where they will not be judged by the color of their skin but by the content of their character.

I have a dream today.

I have a dream that one day the state of Alabama, whose governor's lips are presently dripping with the words of interposition and nullification will be transformed into a situation where little Black boys and Black girls will be able to join hands with little White boys and White girls and walk together as sisters and brothers.

I have a dream today.

I have a dream that one day every valley shall be exalted, every hill and mountain shall be made low, the rough places will be made plains, and the crooked places will be made straight, and the glory of the Lord shall be revealed, and all flesh shall see it together.

This is our hope. This is the faith with which I return to the South. With this faith we will be able to hew out of the mountain of despair a stone of hope. With this faith we will be able to transform the jangling of discords of our nation into a beautiful symphony of brotherhood. With this faith we will be able to work together, to pray together, to struggle together, to go to jail together, to stand up for freedom together, knowing that we will be free one day.

This will be the day when all of God's children will be able to sing with new meaning.

> "My country, 'tis of thee,
> Sweet land of liberty,
>   Of thee I sing:
> Land where my fathers died,
> Land of the pilgrims' pride,
> From every mountain-side
>   Let freedom ring."

And if America is to be a great nation this must become true. So let freedom ring from the prodigious hilltops of New Hampshire. Let freedom ring from the mighty mountains of New York. Let freedom ring from the heightening Alleghenies of Pennsylvania!

Let freedom ring from the snowcapped Rockies of Colorado!
Let freedom ring from the curvacious peaks of California!
But not only that; let freedom ring from Stone Mountain of Georgia!
Let freedom ring from Lookout Mountain of Tennessee!
Let freedom ring from every hill and molehill of Mississippi. From every
mountaintop, let freedom ring.

When we let freedom ring, when we let it ring from every village and every
hamlet, from every state and every city, we will be able to speed up that day
when all of God's children, Black men and White men, Jews and Gentiles, Pro-
testants and Catholics, will be able to join hands and sing in the words of the
old Negro spiritual, "Free at last! free at last! thank God almighty, we are free
at last!"

Although the first-person "I" beginning *is* dramatic and intense, there are
some warnings to be made: If the writer begins with the "I" beginnings, the
article should continue with the "I" form throughout. If the "I" of the narrative somehow disappears in the middle of the narrative, the reader is left
to wonder when the "I" of the writer will reappear. The reader is left waiting
expectantly, like a child waiting for the jack-in-the-box to jump out of a
musical toy. If the "I" of the narrator never reappears, the reader is left
frustrated, wondering—logically—why an article that began with the "I" of
the narrator suddenly shifted away in mid-stream.

Additionally, an article written in the "I" form—although involving—
may be limited to *only what the narrator sees or understands.* Such a narrative may lack the omnipotent point of view that would benefit the reader.

Finally, the "I" or first-person viewpoint, if written in a naive or un-
sophisticated way, may lose readers who are more experienced in the subject.
Or, if an "I" form article is full of the author's galloping egotism, that may
also turn readers away from the writer *and* the story.

Despite the problems with the first-person "I" narrative, there is nothing
more fun than being pulled into a story with the voice of the narrator on
page 1.

My favorite all-time "I" beginning? It's from a long-forgotten book about
carnival life, *Step Right Up!*, written by Dan Mannix, in 1951. (I bought a
water-stained copy for a quarter once because I loved the beginning.) Who
couldn't help but be captivated by this:

I probably never would have become America's leading fire-eater if Flamo the
Great hadn't happened to explode that night in front of Krinko's Great Combined Side Shows. (p. 1)

Now there's a book that literally begins with a bang!

One more "I" beginning, just as fascinating to me, was the beginning of
the article "DeSoto Adventurer II," by Patrick Bedard, from *Car & Driver*
magazine, September, 1987.

Bedard discusses the DeSoto Adventurer II and other "dream cars" of the 1950s—how exciting they seemed to be then—and how oh-so-very-mediocre they appear to be in the 1980s. His beginning:

> I remember the future, plain as yesterday.
>
> Well, I don't remember the whole future—not the food, not the houses, not even the women. But I'll tell you one thing: the cars were really bitchin'.
>
> Everyone who was a car-kook adolescent in the early fifties remembers the same scenario. The cars of the future were really low, and some of them had glass canopies overhead, like the F-86 Sabre's. Even the smallest ones were as long as Cadillacs, and their flamboyant fenders tapered back to jet exhausts. They were fast, too. They had to be, just to keep up with traffic that would average, oh, probably 100 mph. I can't recall anybody saying exactly, but high speeds were definitely baked into the promise of the future.
>
> The America of the fifties loked forward to a utopian future. Optimism had spread from sea to shining sea and hardened like concrete. We'd licked the Nazis and we'd whipped the Japanese. Now there was only one enemy left—the ordinary life—and Yankee ingenuity would triumph over that one, too. Cars were the chosen symbol of the future. We'd ride into this utopian dream in low-slung, transparent-canopied stilettos on wheels. And everybody would be smiling like Ozzie and Harriet. (p. 58)

Name: "I" (first-person) beginning.

Frequency of use: Occasionally seen. Especially appropriate for author-participation material, confessional material.

Length: Varies with subject.

Difficulty range: 5–7.

Advisory. Writer must be aware of limitations of "I" usage throughout the narrative and must be aware of the level of sophistication of the story.

THE "YOU" BEGINNING

"Your child is listless and glassey-eyed"

We read newspapers and magazines because we learn from them—we read expert advice and we learn how to live, how to get better credit, how to raise our families, and how to maintain our homes effectively.

In fact, one of the primary functions of "shelter" magazines such as *Better Homes & Gardens, Family Circle, Prevention,* and even *Mother Earth News,* is a *service* function—teaching readers how to live better.

To do that, writers often begin articles in the "you" form.

This technique speaks directly to the reader, offering guidance and help.

Here is a typical "you" form beginning, from the November, 1986 issue of *Better Homes & Gardens*. The article is titled "Fever: New Facts You Should Know":

> Your child is listless and glassey-eyed, or perhaps your ill spouse is shivering and aching. A hand on the forehead confirms your suspicion of a full-fledged fever. Popping a thermometer into the patient's mouth, you reach for some fever-reducing medication.
>
> Bringing down the fever isn't always the best remedy. A growing number of doctors now say that lowering a fever may prolong the illness, increase contagion, and hamper treatment.
>
> "There is some evidence that fever may be of some benefit," states Dr. Philip Brunell, who chairs the Committee on Infectious Diseases of the American Academy of Pediatrics (AAP). "It is one weapon the body uses to protect itself. Moderate fever is not an enemy. It can usually be allowed to run its course."

Notice how many times the writer, Edwin Kiester, Jr. uses the "you." There is one in the subtitle, and four in the first paragraph.

There is a simple key to this: If you are writing self-help material—medical, psychological, educational or home-and-family material (or other advice)— you can phrase the material mentally, *as if you are talking to a close friend.* Many magazines, particularly, think of themselves as the "friend of the family." *Better Homes & Gardens* uses this line on the top front cover: "The Idea Magazine for American Families." If you write to your readers as you would talk to a friend, you will likely use the "you" (second-person) form. It can be very effective—and is an easy form to use. (I used the "you" in the beginning of this chapter—talking to *you* the reader of this book.)

Name: "You" beginning.

Frequency of use: Often seen.

Length: Varies with material—usually one to three paragraphs or slightly more.

Difficulty range: 1–3. An easy and effective beginning to use.

Advisory. Appropriate and very effective beginning for "help material" (i.e., educational, family, home, guidance, and "support" writing).

THE QUOTATION BEGINNING

"Closest thing to dyin' I know of"

In this beginning, the writer uses a key quotation from the subject of the article to highlight his or her personality.

This is often an exceptional method of beginning a personality profile, for you have the subject of the profile speaking directly to the readers. The quotation should be meaningful, and clear. The quotation must make sense at the beginning of the article, for the reader only has the first page, the headline, subhead (if any), photographs (if any), and the article beginning as orientation.

The more the single quotation highlights the personality, the more effective it is at the beginning of the article.

Here, from *Sport* magazine, Dec., 1986, is an ideal quotation beginning, in an article about retired UCLA basketball coach John Wooden. Wooden, who won more college championships than any other coach, was profiled in an article by John Capouya, titled "John Wooden." The subtitle was "Zen and the art of basketball: In retirement, an old master looks back."

> "The two most important words in life," says John Wooden, "are love and balance. In athletics, it's balance." For 40 years Wooden taught his basketball players to keep their feet spread slightly wider than their shoulders, favored a high-post offense that "forced the defense to cover the entire court" and insisted on team play. The balance he stressed was emotional as well as physical; he liked his teams businesslike rather than inspired. Wooden sought moderation in all things, the happy medium, what Zen Buddhists call the Middle Way.
>
> The result was not harmony but hegemony. In his 27 years at UCLA, Wooden's teams won 620 games (including a record 88 in a row) and lost 147, for an .808 winning percentage. They won seven consecutive NCAA championships, 10 in Wooden's last 12 coaching years. Inexorably efficient, Wooden was seen as an athletic Henry Ford, dominating through organization and discipline, industry and individual initiative. The repetitive practice drills, the conveyor belt of incoming talent—his was success by assembly line.
>
> But in reconsidering Wooden's career and in visiting with him 11 years after his retirement, a sharply different image emerges. Not that everything we knew about Wooden is wrong, only that the reverse is equally true. Now he seems less driven to success by his Western methodology as carried by his Eastern thinking, as much a Zen mystic as an American archetype. That he could productively contain these contradictions is the most Eastern notion, and perhaps the best explanation, of all. (p. 51)

The quotation from the subject does not have to be long or detailed, but it should be significant to be effective. Then the writer can elaborate on it, as Capouya did in this beginning. The writer may explain why the statement is true or perhaps explain why the speaker *believes it to be true.* If the statement is significant, but self-serving, the writer may contradict the statement and may offer proof of why the statement is shaded by self-image or hypocrisy.

Here is an example of a short and concise quotation—used in the opening paragraph of a book review. The review was by David Kelly (1987), editor of *The New York Times Book Review.* His review of Elliott J. Gorn's book *The Manly Art: Bare-Knuckle Prize Fighting in America* appeared in *The New York Times Book Review:*

"Closest thing to dyin' that I know of" was Muhammad Ali's memorable description of the "thrilla in Manila," in which he and Joe Frazier fought 14 fierce, wearying rounds. His words characterize even more fittingly many of the bare-knuckle prizefights Elliott J. Gorn recounts in his exemplary book, "The Manly Art." (p. 8)

Name: Quotation beginning.

Frequency of use: Often seen; especially effective in personality profiles.

Length: Varies with subject. The quotation is usually short, followed by explanation or summary by the writer.

Difficulty range: 2–4. Relatively easy and effective beginning to use.

THE QUESTION BEGINNING

"Who is the top-grossing movie star of all time?"

In this opening, the writer asks a question about the subject the reader should consider. This technique draws the reader into the story, but to be effective, the question should be direct and understandable *and should be answerable by Yes or No.* (Or, in some cases, could be a multiple choice answer.) The writer should avoid asking a metaphysical or highly abstruse question.

The writer can often combine the question beginning with the "you" form, speaking directly to the reader: "How would you, (reader) like to do such-and-such. . . ." or "Do you (reader) think 'A' is true or 'B' is true: ———?"

Here is a multiple choice question beginning, in a *Newsday* story by Mike McGrady (1986), about actor Harrison Ford:

> Today, a small two-part quiz for movie buffs. Who is the top-grossing movie star of all time?
>
> Is it a) Clint Eastwood; b) Charles Bronson; c) Sylvester Stallone; d) Harrison Ford; e) Burt Reynolds; or f) Lassie?
>
> The answer may be a surprise: d.
>
> Harrison Ford's movies have made more money than those of any other actor in history. In fact, no fewer than five of the 10 top-grossing movies of all time have starred Harrison Ford. At this moment, Harrison Ford movies have sold more than a billion dollars worth of tickets.
>
> Now, the second part of this quiz: How do you explain this?
>
> Is it a) dramatic talent; b) skill in selection; c) classic good looks; d) sex appeal or e) luck?
>
> "That's just luck," Ford said. "I don't know how else to relate to it. I choose the best projects that are available and the best people I can work with. The rest of it is luck."

True enough, there have been some lucky moments. When Ford was chosen to star as Han Solo in 1977's *Star Wars,* he was a complete unknown, except to a handful of directors (Stephen Spielberg, George Lucas and Francis Coppola) who had used him in bit parts. Luckily enough, *Star Wars* happened to gross more than $300 million in its first year of release, and that led to two highly profitable spinoffs. It also led to his work in the two Indiana Jones movies (a third will be shot next spring).

Ford now enjoys a near-unique ability to define his own career. Unlike some other stars, he chooses not to be a one-note performer, instead selecting roles of considerable challenge. Recent choices: *Blade Runner* (directed by Ridley Scott), last year's excellent *Witness* (directed by Peter Weir) and the soon-to-be-released *The Mosquito Coast* (also directed by Peter Weir).

Here is another example of the question beginning, in an article about bulldozers, in the February, 1987 issue of *Car and Driver* magazine. Written by Executive Editor Rich Ceppos, the article was titled "Make the Earth Move" and was subtitled "All it takes is a hard hat and a Caterpillar D8N."

Have you ever felt like gouging a piece out of New Jersey and adding it onto New York? Have you ever felt a need to adjust the height of the Rockies? Any interest in digging a hole the size of Shea Stadium? You've come to the right place.

And if you're one of those purists who want to read only about shimmering technology and form-follows-function engineering, don't turn the page just yet, because we've got something for you as well. How about a turbocharged, 14.6-liter six-cylinder diesel that produces 977 pound-feet of torque and can run flat out all day long?

Not enough? What do you say to a 770-hp, twin-turbo, 34.5-liter V-8 bolted into a machine that is twice the size of a Sherman tank, decked out with power assists and air conditioning and so agile that it can spin pirouettes like Walter Payton evading the defense?

We're talking manly, brawny stuff here, like rocks and boulders and dirt and dust, monstrous machines, hard hats and sweat, plaid shorts and beer. We're talking about making the earth move, partner.

We have the Caterpillar folks to thank for showing us how—and then some. All we asked for was a simple test drive of their hot new D8N crawler tractor (that's "bulldozer" to you greenhorns), but before the day is done we'll be treated to a trip through hard-hat heaven. (p. 67)

Here's another interesting question beginning, from an article moved on *The Chicago Tribune* wire service in January, 1987:

Is Mike Ditka one of the more blunt-spoken evangelists of America's true folk religion? Is Walter Payton a living saint of our national faith? And is the Super Bowl the ritual revival service for believers and skeptics alike?

The answer, brothers and sisters, appears to be a resounding yes, by the reckoning of James A. Mathisen, a sociologist at Wheaton College in Illinois.

Mathisen, in a scholarly paper presented at the annual meeting of the Society for the Scientific Study of Religion argued that the Super Bowl has become "the American spectacle of folk religion . . . the festival of the folk, (celebrating) their faith, their practice and their history."

That view of sports as religion and professional football as its leading sectarian expression is not a new notion, but one that has achieved growing currency among American scholars and cultural critics.

Sports have become the sacramental expression for the American way of life, these observers contend, and have emerged as the common religion of the land.

Of course, one of the most quoted question beginnings of all time is Elizabeth Barrett Browning's poem:

> How do I love thee?
> Let me count the ways. . . .

Reciting this old poem is probably the only time most Americans use the word *thee*.

Name: Question beginning.

Frequency of use: Often seen.

Length: Varies with subject.

Difficulty range: 3–4. Relatively easy, if the writer remembers to ask a question that is understandable, that can be answered with either a yes or no, or multiple choice, and that is clear and reasonable.

THE PARODY BEGINNING

"Call me Jonah"

In this beginning, the writer uses a well-known joke, slogan, or phrase, but alters it for his or her own use. During the Reagan–Mondale election, the Wendy's hamburger chain gained "market share" with a series of commercials with senior citizen Clara Peller, who inspected a fast food burger and demanded "Where's the beef?"

The phrase was so popular that Walter Mondale repeated it in reference to Reagan's proposed first-year budget. It was a hit during Mondale appearances.

That's an ideal parody beginning.

The warning here is that the writer should use a phrase that is so widely known that the writer can expect readers will know where it came from—what the original line was.

Will Hampton, staff writer for *The Daily Texan,* the student newspaper of the University of Texas at Austin, used a Parody Beginning Nov. 12, 1986, in describing the last weeks of the 1986 football season, in the Southwest Conference:

> Maybe the Southwest Conference should apply for a Mastercard. Talk about needing to master the possibilities.
>
> Going into the 12th week of the season, four teams—almost half the conference—are still in contention for the Cotton Bowl. In order of probability they are: Texas A & M, Arkansas, Baylor and Texas.
>
> The Longhorns must beat Baylor in Waco Saturday and Texas A & M at home on Thanksgiving and have SMU upset No. 11 Arkansas to make it to the Cotton Bowl. Kickoff for Arkansas-SMU is 2 p.m. Saturday in Texas Stadium.
>
> The Aggies can simplify matters by winning their last two games, against TCU and Texas, to clinch their second consecutive SWC crown. The Razorbacks need to beat SMU Saturday and have Texas A & M lose once to go to the Cotton Bowl for the first time in 10 years.
>
> Baylor needs to beat Texas Saturday and have the Aggies lose twice to spend New Year's Day in Dallas. (p. 13)

Staff writer Greg Stoda (1986), in *The Dallas Times Herald,* used the catchphrase from the TV show "The Price is Right" as he began his story in *The Times Herald* about a possible "out of area" opponent for a Cotton Bowl bid:

> Washington Huskies, come on down, you're the next contestant on the Cotton Bowl list.
>
> Cotton Bowl officials will see six games Saturday in an attempt to begin making their decision on an at-large team for the New Year's Day game. Bowl bids will be issued Nov. 22.
>
> "That might mean one or two more than usual for this time of year, but we've got to keep all our options open until this Penn State-Miami thing is resolved," said Jim "Hoss" Brock, Cotton Bowl executive vice president.
>
> The possibility still exists that Penn State and Miami, two unbeaten independents, could arrange their own national championship showdown in the Citrus Bowl or Fiesta Bowl on New Year's Day. As long as that's the case, Brock and the Cotton Bowl are scrambling.
>
> All the way to Seattle, where Washington, ranked 10th by The Associated Press, plays at home against UCLA. (p. C1)

The parody beginning can be more than just a television or advertising slogan, however. Here is Kurt Vonnegut Jr.'s beginning to his 1963 novel, *Cat's Cradle:*

> Call me Jonah. My parents did, or mostly did. They called me John.
>
> Jonah—John—if I had been a Sam, I would have been a Jonah still—not because I have been unlucky for others, but because somebody or something

has compelled me to be certain places at certain times, without fail. Conveyances and motives, both conventional and bizarre, have been provided. And, according to plan, at each appointed second, at each appointed place, this Jonah was there. (p. 13)

It seems to me that there is more than just a touch of Melville's Ishmael in Vonnegut's opening.

Paul B. Carroll (1987), staff reporter of *The Wall Street Journal,* varied that slightly for the beginning of an article about the perils of a landlubber on the high seas. *The Journal* headlined his article "Landlubber Reporter Sails the Atlantic And Survives, Barely." (*The Wall Street Journal* also placed the article in the fourth-from-the-left-side, front-page column that they reserve for their "oddity story of the day.")

> Call me Schlemiel.
> With just two days' sailing experience, I blithely accepted a friend's invitation to join the crew on a 42-foot sailboat in the transatlantic Constitution Race, which began May 16.
> It seemed like a good idea at the time.
> Starting my first watch at 3 a.m. in the English Channel, however, I wasn't so certain. As I stepped into the cockpit, the first mate told me: "If you go overboard, the water is so cold you'll only last 15 minutes, and in the dark we'll never find you. If you go overboard, just take a couple of big gulps of water and go under. You'll save yourself a lot of time and trouble."
> As the 4,000-mile trip progressed across the North Atlantic, we sailed into two weeks of storms so severe they nearly banged the boat apart. The bulkheads cracked, and the sails tore. Most ominous, the mast seemed to be pounding its way through the bottom of the hull as we were 1,500 miles from the U.S., heading into our third gale in less than a week and unable to raise help on the radio. (p. 1).

Here's a parody beginning, using the famous monologue from the original "The Twilight Zone" series by Rod Serling. This was the lead from an article "Small Screen's Big Credits" by Harry F. Waters with Lee Goldberg in Los Angeles, published in *Newsweek* magazine Oct. 14, 1985.

> *You're traveling through another dimension, a dimension not only of sight and sound but of mind, a journey into a 19-inch land whose boundaries are those of imbecility, timidity, mimicry and mediocrity . . .*
> OK, Rod Serling wouldn't go that far: He *liked* working in television almost as much as we loved "The Twilight Zone." But there's no disputing that the late Serling's appreciation for the medium was never shared by Hollywood's top-of-the-line moviemakers. To them, TV's weekly series format, with its familiar characters doing predictable things, has traditionally represented a creative void that some quickly passed through on their way to cinematic respectability and others simply shunned. How is it, a viewer of the fall season might wonder,

that prime time suddenly finds itself blessed with the services of such big-name directors as Steven Spielberg, Brian DePalma, Michael Crichton, Clint Eastwood, John
Milius, William Friedkin and Martin Scorcese? (p. 99)

Austin, Texas *American-Statesman* film critic Patrick Taggart used a parody
of Biblical prose to review the film *King David*. His review appeared March
30, 1985, under the headline " 'King David' film just rolls over and plays dead."

> *And lo a decree went out that Australian directors should journey to the
> land called Hollywood, there to continue their art, enjoying the riches of the
> promised land and six-figure salaries.*
>   *And Bruce Beresford did go to the place called Waxahachie, where in green
> pastures he fashioned the testament called "Tender Mercies," the passionate
> story of a simple man, and there was great rejoicing.*
>   *And Peter Weir did in like manner jet his way to the mountains of Penn-
> sylvania and begat "Witness," and again there was great rejoicing.*
>   *And Bruce Beresford, now a shepard of a large flock and a budget worthy
> of a philistine king, did go to the Holy Land for the film of "King David."
> And when the light shown upon the king's countenance he was Richard Gere,
> and again there was great rejoicing.*
>   *But then the film was finished and this week released, and there was, as some
> prophets had warned, much renting of garments and gnashing of teeth. The
> public who had crossed many miles for the sneak preview laughed as one, and
> said: "Thou wilt look away."*
>   In other words, Beresford's *King David* is a dog that howls long and loud
> into the night. Sometimes good intentions aren't enough, and Beresford's com-
> mendable goal of creating a warts-and-all Bible epic in which characters would
> behave more credibly than in Cecile B. DeMille's creations of the 1950s isn't
> met. (p. 44)

Here's another nice parody beginning: Jody Conradt, women's basketball
coach for the University of Texas Lady Longhorns has been so successful that
in 10 years her teams have never lost a Southwest Conference game. In 1986,
her team won every game for a 34-0 record and the national championship.

In mid-March, 1988, she approached her 500th victory and, as she did so,
the pressure became enormous. Jerry Gernander (1988), writing in *The Daily
Texan,* used a nice parody lead in a story which was headlined "Conradt shoots
for 500th victory Saturday":

> *"Just say no."*
> Jody Conradt heard the whispers, grudgingly. Women's Athletic Director
> Donna Lopiano warned her she was doing too much; she need to cut back.
>   *"Just say no."*
> The appreciation Conradt felt toward women's basketball fans, who were
> scarce a decade ago, led her to accept all requests for speeches and appearances.
>   *"Just say no."*

Finally, she consented. She does not exactly have it easy now. But Jody Conradt, in her 12th year as the Lady Longhorns' head coach and aiming for her 500th career coaching victory Saturday, is at least living a manageable life again.

"This year, I made the resolution I just had to say no some," Conradt said. "I don't like to do that. I reached a point [of] the absolute maximum. Saying no is not easy."

But sometimes it is necessary. During the off-season, Conradt makes several speaking apperances per week. She still tries to answer all correspondence. Autograph requests take time. And besides all that, she is in the midst of putting together one of the nation's best recruiting classes and pushing the current team toward the Final Four.

All the work, through 18 years of coaching, has paid off. Conradt may be the most popular—and busiest—woman in Austin.

"If the public were Catholic, she'd be pope," Lopiano said.

The pontiff could use Conradt's stamina. (p. 1)

PS: Jody Conradt got her 500th victory as expected. Her Lady Longhorns beat the Texas Tech Lady Red Raiders 88–61.

Name: Parody beginning.

Frequency of use: Seen occasionally.

Length: Varies with subject, but is usually short—a paragraph or so.

Difficulty level: 3–5. If the writer is working with a deadline—on a newspaper—the parody line may appear in the writer's imagination an hour *after the day's deadline*. In short, it may be difficult to fit in a parody beginning at a moment's notice.

Advisory.   For the parody to be effective, the original line must usually be current enough so the audience will recognize the parody.

THE "CLASSIFIED AD" BEGINNING

"Politically dead: James Watt, 45"

If you are stuck for a terrific beginning and nothing comes to mind, what do you do? The blank sheet of paper in your typewriter stares back at you, or the blinking cursor on your word processor mocks you. What do you do? You look through writing guidebooks, if you have any close to your desk. You might browse through a magazine or the front page of the daily newspaper, hoping to find a similar article you can copy a lead from. But if that is all you do, you may miss a treasure of possibilities in the classified advertising pages of the paper, especially if you have a large metropolitan daily paper in hand.

Look at the vast number of categories:

Obituaries
Automobiles for sale
Trucks, heavy equipment, trailers, mobile homes for sale
Aircraft for sale, parts, service
Campers, recreational vehicles, travel trailers, leasing
Birth announcements
Entertainment notices
Hunting/fishing notices
Lodges, (Elks, Rotary, etc.) meetings
Lost & Found
Child-care services
Cemetary lots
Music, musicians to book
Escort services
Personals
Business notices
Massage, health & fitness services
Schools & colleges
Trade schools
Loans, or wanted to borrow
Stocks, bonds
Investment opportunities
Appliance repair
Attorneys
Computer services
Electrical services
Exterminators
Remodeling, furniture repair

And the list goes on and on and on:

Domestic, household help wanted
Medical
Dental help wanted
Sales help wanted
Part-time opportunities
Garage sales (sometimes called "tag sales" in various parts of the country).

Merchandise of all kinds for sale: art objects, antiques, appliances, bicycles, boats, computers, cameras, children's items, china, food products, collector's items, guns and ammunition, jewelry, stereos and TVs, and sporting goods.

Livestock: dogs for sale, dogs lost, dogs found, cats for sale, cats lost, cats found, farm livestock, horses, cattle, birds, pet supplies, feed, grain, breeding services.

Rentals: homes, apartments, condos (furnished or unfurnished, semi-furnished, daily, weekly, monthly). Duplexes: mobile homes for rent, roommates wanted.

Land for sale, homes for sale, business space for rent, for lease, for sale, acreages, ranch property.

If you look through these categories, you may be able to rewrite or revise a standard classified ad into an ingenious beginning for your article.

This *is* a parody technique and can be used only occasionally, but it can be wry and effective.

How can this technique be used?

You can "play it straight" with a real-sounding advertisement or use a satiric form.

Early in the Reagan administration, the resignation of James Watt allowed *Newsweek* to use a revised obituary beginning in a story about the last days of Watt:

> Politically dead: James Watt, 45, controversial secretary of the interior from 1981 to 1983; in Washington after a brief but devastating bout of the dread disease known as Potomac hoof-in-mouth. A darling of the Republican right and a hero to Sagebrush rebels in the west, Watt contracted his fatal infection after joking about a government study commission composed of "a black, a woman, two Jews and a cripple." He never regained consciousness.

Columnist Erma Bombeck used a similar beginning in a April 1988 column that appeared in some newspapers under the title "No one mourns the demise of the mini":

> It was such a small death notice, you may have missed it. "SKIRT, MINI, age 12 months, died of public apathy complicated by dissent as it slept on clothing racks throughout the country. Only a small group of mourners (12 male designers and 15 starved models) were on hand to mark the passing. Plans are being made by 11 states to declare the first Monday in April a paid legal holiday."
>
> I hate to speak ill of the dead, but I thought miniskirts would never go. I was ready to pull the life-support systems on them last fall when I saw them in store windows. They were designed for failure. One simply cannot compress an active body with 162 movable parts, layered with cellulite and love handles

from excessive eating, into a small square the size of a heating pad and expect women to go out in public in it.

It was not what you would call the love affair of the century. Television personalities clung to their desks as if they were life preservers on the Titanic. Laws were passed in some states saying you had to be 18 to watch a woman get in and out of her car. I know two women who gave up climbing stairs for Lent. The struggle with short skirts was not a pretty sight.

Note that if the article is a long one, and t he classified ad beginning is short, the writer must somehow bridge the gap between the end of the classified ad beginning and the rest of the text. A spacebreak (see the section on Transitions) is most effective here.

Name: Classified ad beginning.

Frequency of use: Seen occasionally.

Length: Varies, but usually short—the same size as a real classified ad.

Difficulty range: 3–4.

Advisory.   This beginning could be set typographically so it appears more like a real advertisement—centered at the top of the article—or perhaps set in "classified ad"-sized type to aid the impact of the beginning.

THE PARADOXICAL BEGINNING

"It was the best of times, it was the worst of times"

This beginning states a problem, or perhaps a paradox, which will be solved later in the article. This can be an intriguing beginning because the writer tantalizes the reader with an unexpected problem, paradox or, more commonly, a contradiction.

This can be fictional in nature, or can be based in fact.

Do you recall the first sentence from George Orwell's *1984*?

It was a bright cold day in April, and the clocks were striking thirteen.

(Also, on the first page, Orwell tells us that an elevator in "Victory Mansions" was not working because "It was part of the economy drive in preparation for Hate Week.")

Just like we recognize Melville's "Call me Ishmael" beginning segment in *Moby Dick,* so we also recognize the beginning in Charles Dickens' *A Tale of Two Cities*:

It was the best of times, it was the worst of times, it was the age of wisdom, it was the age of foolishness, it was the epoch of belief, it was the epoch of incredulity, it was the season of Light, it was the season of Darkness, it was the spring of hope, it was the winter of despair, we had everything before us, we had nothing before us, we were all going direct to heaven, we were all direct the other way—in short, the period was so far like the present period, that some of its noisiest authorities insisted on its being received, for good or evil, in the superlative degree of comparison only.

That beginning is perhaps the most famous "contradictory" beginning in all literature.

And writers use contradictory beginnings all the time. Richard Stengel (1986), writing in *Time,* used such a beginning in an article in *Time*'s "The Nation" section, under a headline "How Reagan Stays Out of Touch":

Serene. Instinctive. Visionary. Determined. Eternally optimistic. Such adjectives are regularly used to form a word picture of Ronald Reagan. They are all true, as far as they go. But each has a less sunny flip side, like a photographic negative of the bright familiar image. Serene: intellectually passive. Instinctive: unreflective. Visionary: oblivious to troubling details. Determined: rigid. Optimistic: detached from reality and unwilling to wrestle with complex issues.

The events surrounding the Iran arms deal reveal how disengaged Ronald Reagan is from the operation of his government, a Chief Executive who is not only uninformed but chooses not to know what is going on in his name. For many close observers of Reagan, the surprise is not that his passive approach has got him into trouble, but that such a fiasco did not happen sooner.

The phrase "Reagan is not a detail man" is a mantra among Reaganites and suggests that he sees the big picture, that "details" are for smaller minds. Yet such detachment can prove dangerous. In preparation for the Iceland summit, Reagan did not study the history and nuances of America's arms-control strategies; instead he practiced ways to sell Gorbachev on SDI. To get himself into the right frame of mind, he read Tom Clancy's *Red Storm Rising,* a potboiler about a non-nuclear war between NATO and the Soviet bloc. On a political trip the day before he left for Iceland, Reagan passed his time aboard Air Force One chatting with Secret Service agents. He negotiated with Gorbachev on instinct. His approach could have led to the type of breakthrough that happens only when leaders sweep aside details and discuss the big picture. Or it could have ended hopes for a limited agreement on European missiles and the use of Star Wars as a bargaining tool. In retrospect, the latter may have occurred.

Reagan's election was a reaction to the micromanagement style of Jimmy Carter, who made it his business to know everything from the fine print in the Pentagon budget to who was playing on the White House tennis court. Reagan, by contrast, has practiced a kind of Zen presidency; the less he worried and prepared, the more popular and effective he would be. (p. 34)

And again, from *Sport* magazine, here is a contradictory beginning by writer Wilfrid Sheed (1986), in an article titled "Branch Ricky." The article's subtitle was: "He revolutioned baseball. Twice. And he was a penny-pinching, scheming hustler of a saint, too."

> Outside of the works of Mark Twain, you have never met anyone like him. Branch Rickey was variously known as the preacher, the deacon, the Mahatma (after Gandhi) and, less formally, the pious fraud.
>
> Although he looked like a minister who would cheat his own flock at bingo, Rickey was not *exactly* a fraud. He was genuinely pious enough not to play ball himself on Sundays, thus shortening his (only so-so) catching career, but he was hustler enough to make thousands out of the concept of the Sunday doubleheader. He had the genuine moral courage to break the color line by bring Jackie Robinson into baseball, but he also had the showmanship to see a fortune that was to be made out of black players and inner-city fans. And this man of God has a special soft spot for sinners like Leo Durocher and the famous Gas House Gang; he even did his bit to pass on stories about them.
>
> Rickey is probably best remembered today for the Great Robinson Breakthrough, but it wasn't the first time that the old boy had revolutionized baseball. Besides such minor innovations as the batting cage and the sliding pit, he introduced a little something called the farm system which changed the whole structure of the game overnight in the Twenties.
>
> It was Rickey's novel notion to start buying up whole teams in the minor leagues rather than one player at a time, thus guaranteeing a huge pool of young talent to call upon at will. The result was immediately dubbed Rickey's chain gang, and the people in it were called Rickey's slaves. But for better or worse it brought the indigent St. Louis Cardinals an on-again, off-again dynasty for a good twenty years, from 1926 to 1946, and it soon had all the other big league teams scrambling to acquire their very own slaves and chain gangs. (p. 29)

Time magazine's cover story for their issue of Jan. 18, 1988 was "Magician of the Musical," a profile of British composer Andrew Lloyd Webber. The story, was subtitled "Lloyd Webber scores again with Phantom." *Time*'s story, written by Michael Walsh (reported by Mary Cronin and others), began:

> *All right, gentlemen, we all agree there is nothing wrong with the Broadway musical that a few hits wouldn't cure. But what we need is some new ideas.*
> O.K., how about this: long-haired hippie from working-class family in ancient Palestine (salt of the earth dad, saintly mom) falls in with tough crowd of longshoremen, starts proletarian pacifist movement and gets offed by protofascist pigs from Rome.
> *Never work: too depressing, and it lacks an upbeat ending. No love interest either. Next?*
> Spunky Argentine firecracker from wrong side of tracks rides casting couch to boffo b.o. in Buenos Aires, weds political top dog, rips off nation, gets cancer and dies.
> *Are you kidding? Too depressing, lacks an upbeat ending, and no one has ever paid a nickel to see anything about South America. Next?*
> Well, there's the one about cats singing poetry . . .

Forget it; pigs will fly first. Ditto your other crazy notion, the one about the roller-skating trains. What else?

Ugly guy who hangs out in basement of Paris Opéra gets crush on cute chorister, secretly preps her as headliner, goes berserk when boyfriend comes on scene, writes opera with her in lead, gets ditched by girl and crawls into hole to die.

Not too bright, man. Depressing, lacks an upbeat ending, and the opera-house setting is a major turnoff. Broadway audiences are not about to put out big bucks to watch a downer like that, for crying out loud. Doesn't anybody here have an idea for a hit musical?

Try this one: shy middle-class British kid grows up listening to Mozart and Richard Rodgers, teams with buddy to write school musical, is discovered by slumming music critic, goes on to pen smash biblical epic *Jesus Chris Superstar* and monster hit *Evita,* splits with pal, has megatriumphs with *Cats* and *Starlight Express,* then comes up with extra-hot spook, *The Phantom of the Opera.* Along the way swaps bell-bottoms for swank Belgravia flat, 1,350-acre English country estate, choice property on the French Riviera, $6 million apartment in Manhattan, private jet, beautiful second wife and a worldwide musical empire that, conservatively, rings his personal cash register to the tune of $12 million a year.

Hmmm. Talent, friendship, strife, love interest, money—it seems to have everything. Now there's uplift for you! We'll call it Andrew Lloyd Webber and His Amazing Technicolor Career. *I think we've got a winner!* (p. 54)

If you begin with a problem or paradoxical beginning, or a contradictory one, you should be prepared to offer the reader one of two choices, later in the article:

- Your own idea of what the solution is. After all, you are, essentially, phrasing this story *like a murder mystery:* You pose a problem first (the dead body on the floor) and offer a solution *later* (the butler did it).
- OR: you should offer enough evidence to allow the reader to make up his or her own mind about the contradictory nature of the story.

Does Ronald Reagan govern effectively or does he "stay out of touch" with the realities of his presidency? Read the entire article in *Time* and decide.

Was Branch Rickey a saint or was he a pious fraud? Read Wilfred Sheen's complete article then decide.

Name: Paradoxical beginning.

Frequency of use: Seen occasionally.

Length: Varies with subject.

Difficulty range: 5–8. Not all stories will present a subject that can be pictured in a paradoxical or contradictory style. Nor may many writers recognize sufficient contradictions to use them in the beginning.

THE COMPARISON OR CONTRAST BEGINNING

"Dr. Jekyll has a master's degree"

If there are two distinct sides or facets to a personality, you may wish to begin your writing by showing these sides—comparing them for the reader or contrasting them.

The Austin, Texas, area is perhaps second only to Nashville in the quantity and quality of country music and rock 'n' roll, with Willie Nelson, George Strait, Stevie Ray Vaughn, and many others calling the Austin area home. Many others either pass through Austin for a one-night stand, or had lived in Austin before moving elsewhere.

The Austin *American-Statesman* writer who covered country music until late 1987 was John T. Davis. Here he profiled musician George Frayne, in an article that was published Oct. 16, 1986. Davis used a perfect comparison beginning:

A Brush With Art
Sensitive painter George Frayne
still rocks as Commander Cody

Dr. Jekyll has a master's degree in fine art, is a student of cinematography, and has a short feature in the Museum of Modern Art's permanent video archives in New York. His oversize paintings, featuring (as one art galley described) "images of contemporary culture presented in a photorealistic manner," have become collector's items. He is a man at home in the temples of high culture that dot the landscape.

Mr. Hyde, on the other hand, is a cigar-chomping wild man in a Hawaiian shirt. Raising his shaggy-maned head to bay at the moon, he flings his hands across the piano keys, scattering boogie-woogie riffs like bursts of shrapnel. Sweat pouring, fingers flying, he evokes a demented response from the midnight ramblers who pack the gin mills and beer joints to which his calling takes him. His songs are paeans to fast times, big trucks, loose ladies and strong drink. He doesn't hang around too many art museums.

Nonetheless, as tradition would have it, Jekyll and Hyde are the same man. The acclaimed artist is George Frayne. His piano-pounding doppleganger is the central figure of Commander Cody and His Lost Planet Airmen (the revised edition bill itself simply as Commander Cody). (p. D1)

How charming Davis's style is: mixing country music, Jekyll-and-Hyde and the words *doppleganger* and *paeans* in the same three paragraphs.

If you have a subject with two separate personalities, or a straight personality and a *doppleganger,* you may consider the comparison or contrast beginning; *or* if you have two distinct personalities, you may wish to use this technique.

Name: Comparison or contrast beginning.

Frequency of use: Seen occasionally.

Length: Varies, but could be constructed with an "A" paragraph and "B" paragraph then a summary paragraph, or an "A" section and a "B" section, then a summary.

Difficulty range: 3–6.

THE LITERARY REFERENCE BEGINNING

"With apologies to Thomas Wolfe"

This technique allows the writer to refer to a famous literary quotation, book, title, or reference. If done well, this adds an extra dimension to the beginning, which the reader may not expect—but will be grateful to find.

In this story, *Austin American-Statesman* staff sportswriter Kirk Bohls (1986) concentrates on an upcoming game between the Aggies of Texas A & M University and Louisiana State University. The game is to be played in Louisiana; the Aggie traveling squad contains 10 Louisiana-born players, returning to their home state to face a hostile crowd. The headline was: "Fighting at home." and the subhead was: "Louisiana-born Aggies return to face LSU." Bohls' opening:

> COLLEGE STATION—With apologies to Thomas Wolfe, several Texas A & M university players believe they can go home again. Whether they live to tell about it is a whole 'nother story.
>
> Ten Louisiana-born Aggies among them starting running back Keith Woodside and offensive guard Jerry Fontenot, are returning to their home state this weekend when A & M visits LSU in both teams' season-opener Saturday night.
>
> But these Aggies aren't nostalgic so much as narrow-minded, at least in purpose. They want to humble LSU in LSU. These transplanted Cajuns are already ragin'.
>
> "I want to score—bad," Woodside says. "There's no telling what I'll do (afterward). But I might catch a whiskey bottle. They have some pretty violent fans after they get a little tipsy." (p. D1)

Dave Dorr (1982) used a key quotation from Dylan Thomas to introduce an article about college basketball star Mark Alcorn, dying of cancer. Dorr's story appeared in *The St. Louis Post-Dispatch*:

> *Do not go gentle*
> *Into that good night.*
> *Rage, rage against*
> *The dying of the light.*
> —Dylan Thomas

He did, with all the fibers in his body. He had felt a concentration of will, a surge of strength, very quickly after those awful moments on a December day 14 months ago when he and his parents were told by a physician that he had a rare form of cancer.

The prognosis then was chilling. He was told he had 90 days to live. If he felt cheated, he did not say so. If he was angered by his helplessness, he kept it to himself.

He promised himself he would maintain his dignity and his self-esteem. He would not back off from a fight; he never had before. He was confident he could master this disease and he would do it quietly—privately—because that was his way.

Each day became a bonus and in his eyes and in his smile you could guess what he was thinking: "who knows what's going to happen to me? I might make it and I might not. But I've got today, this day, and I'm going to make it count."

An athlete, he knew his body. The fight that he was fighting made him and those around him acutely aware of the joy of living, of how precious life is.

Mark Alcorn stretched himself and his capacity to endure, particularly so in the last months when there was so little respite from the pain.

There are other possibilities to this technique as well. There is no limitation on what the reference might be, as long as it is appropriate to the story. Here, author Dirk Hanson (1982) used an ingenuous reference to an early Dustin Hoffman film to begin the introduction to his book, *The New Alchemists: Silicon Valley and the Micro-Electronics Revolution:*

> "Plastics," a well-meaning elder whispered to young Benjamin in *The Graduate*. It was sound enough financial advice, but "silicon" would have been closer to the mark. Forty miles south of San Francisco, in a place known as Silicon Valley, the blueprints of the technological future are being etched on tiny slivers of crystalline silicon. Microelectronics—the science of creating thousands of solid-state electronic elements on a silicon chip—is the hidden foundation of modern technology, and it is changing how we live, work and interact with others in ways even the architects of the transformation do not fully understand. (p. xi)

An anonymous Associated Press writer used the famous McDonald's advertising line in the beginning of a story about how Joan Kroc, the widow of McDonald's founder Ray Kroc, had donated $1 million to the national Democratic party. This wire story appeared in *The Austin American-Statesman* Friday, August 14, 1987 under the headline: "Fast-Food Widow Gives $1 Million to Democrats."

> WASHINGTON (AP)—Joan Kroc, widow of the McDonald's fast-food magnate, is telling Democrats "you deserve a break today." She announced Thursday she has given them $1 million, the biggest single contribution in party history.

Kroc, a registered independent and an advocate of nuclear disarmament, said the contribution was motivated by concern about the direction the nation has taken during the Reagan administration.

She said she is looking to the Democrats "for the positive, principled leadership we must have to restore America to its proper place as the foremost champion of peace and justice in the world." (p. A5)

Perhaps the most famous literary reference beginning ever written is Grantland Rice's (1924) lead for his story of the Notre Dame-Army football game. His beginning:

Outlined against a blue, grey October sky the Four Horsemen rode again.

In dramatic lore they are known as famine, pestilence, destruction and death. These are only aliases. Their real names are: Stuhldreher, Miller, Crowley and Layden. They formed the crest of the South Bend cyclone before which another fighting Army team was swept over the precipice at the Polo Grounds this afternoon as 55,000 spectators peered down upon the bewildering panorama spread out upon the green plain below.

(Somewhat later sportswriter Red Smith, less than impressed with this style asked "where was Grantland Rice to see them 'outlined against a blue, grey sky' " Smith and other sportswriters covered football from the pressbox, high *over* the stadium. Smith's thoughtful answer: Rice was on the sidelines, belly down on the ground, looking at the game with his face pressed sideways on the grass.)

Here is a nicely crafted Literary Reference beginning, using an old proverb. This article, titled "Upwardly Mobile" was written by Candace Beaver and appeared in *The Daily Texan,* at The University of Texas at Austin, Feb. 11, 1987.

An old American Indian proverb says you cannot know a man until you have walked a mile in his moccasins.

If that is true, Bill Perry is not an easy man to know.

Perry's moccasins are comfortable enough to put on. He wears normal, everyday running shoes.

But Perry's shoes are attached to artificial legs.

And he does not walk miles. He runs them.

Perry competed with almost 100 athletes in Austin Saturday in the One American Center Stairclimb. His was not the fastest finishing time in the 32-story race, but it is hard to say he was not a winner. The 40-year-old father of three is one of only a handful of wheelchair athletes who have made the almost superhuman transition form wheelchair competition to racing on foot.

Since April 1985 Perry has competed in almost every type of wheelchair event imaginable—5K runs to marathons, bowling, tennis, shooting and even pentathlon. He went with the U.S. National Shooting Team to Puerto Rico last fall for the Pan American International Wheelchair Games. He came back with four gold and three bronze medals. (p. 10)

Here's a charming beginning from an article titled "Visions of Max Headroom: A Warning About the Future of Higher Education," written by Martin Kellman (1987) and published in *The Chronicle of Higher Education:*

> One evening, like Coleridge, I awoke from a dream, which in my case was brought on by a rerun of *Moonlighting*. The vision I confronted—*Max Headroom: 20 Minutes into the Future*—was as disturbing as "Kubla Khan." The images on the screen flashed like fireflies on a moonless night, and I was in their thrall. Like most futurist fantasies, *Max Headroom* is a warning; unlike much television fare, it is very well done. I remained to scoff; now I come to pray for us all.
>
> Max is a household name among college students, and he is deemed strong enough by Coke to do battle with Pepsi's Lionel Richie and Michael Jackson. A *Newsweek* cover story completed his apotheosis. His name is known to 76 per cent of all teenagers, many more than can identify George Bush. As Max would say, in his electronic stutter, "I am an im-im-image whose ti-ti-time has come."
>
> Who is Max and what is he? Max is the computerized projection of an aggressive reporter named Edison (old technology) Carter, who might have died in a confrontation with a barrier labeled "Max. Headroom 2.3 m." if it hadn't been for a 14-year-old hacker who saved his life by putting his psyche on software. Carter works for the dominant TV network, where Max resides in the network computer, popping up on TV screens in controlled and uncontrolled modes.
>
> Max serves as a floating verbal id, saying all the things that Edison dares only to think. His comments about the programs he introduces and interrupts are coolly cynical—he often imitates Bogart—and are delivered with a stammer that is the product of hasty programming. Unlike Demosthenes or Moses, charismatic figures with speech defects, he is too paralyzed by Weltschmerz to lead.
>
> The future depicted in the show is a frightening cultural wasteland. Instead of countries competing for territories or markets, the dominant cultural entities are networks competing for ratings in a war in which all is fair. In the opening episode, the network invents "blipverts," intense, 15-second ads that viewers will not zap. The blipverts, which resemble real ads, have such concentrated imagery that they actually blow up "couch potatoes." One network signs a contract with terrorists for exclusive live coverage of their revolutionary acts, which terrorists then simulate.
>
> In this post-Orwellian vision . . . (p. B1)

Finally, here is a fine beginning by *Time* magazine staff writer Lance Morrow (1987) from a cover article simply titled "Africa."

> The animals stand motionless in gold-white grasses—zebras and impala, Thomson's gazelles and Cape buffalo and hartebeests and waterbuck and giraffes, and wildebeasts by the thousands, all fixed in art naif, in a smiting equatorial light. They stand in the shadowless clarity of creation.

Now across the immense African landscape, from the distant escarpment, a grey-purple rainstorm blows. It encroaches upon the sunlight, moving through the air like a dark idea. East Africa has a genius for such moments. Wildlife and landscape here have about them a force of melodrama and annunciation. They are the *Book of Genesis* enacted as an afternoon dream.

My own favorite literary reference opening? It is by Tony Kornheiser (1986) in *Sport* magazine (and if I give you the article title, I give away the opening). Kornheiser wrote:

> The Bible acquaints us with the prophet Jeremiah, a righteous man lamenting the evil, decay and disaster around him, predicting calamity for those who won't heed his words. Scolding, chiding, on yet another crusade and pumped full of self-aggrandizing scholasticism. Just who does Jeremiah think he is?
> Close your eyes and listen: This is How-wuhd Co-sell speaking of sports. (p. 59)

Marvelous! Just marvelous! (The article title was simply "Howard Cosell.")

Name: Literary reference beginning.

Frequency of use: Seen occasionally.

Length: Varies.

Difficulty range: 5–7.

Advisory.   Writers should begin with fresh, interesting, valuable material. The more banal, the more cliché-ridden, the less effective the opening less better. Like fruit and vegetables at the supermarket, fresher is better.

THE SIMILE OR METAPHOR BEGINNING

"Folk artists are like wild flowers"

A simile is a comparison of two separate objects with the word *like*. A metaphor is the same comparison *without the word like*. Both can offer the writer ingenious beginnings, if carefully planned.

Here, *Austin American-Statesman* television critic Diane Holloway (1987) used a simile opening in her column. The headline and subhead were:

Tough guys
Telly Savalas, Vince Edwards Reprise Roles
of "Kojak" and "Ben Casey"

> LOS ANGELES—Television actors are a lot like old clothes. If you keep them around long enough, they'll eventually come back in style.

Two old suits recently taken out of mothballs are Telly Savalas and Vince Edwards. They're getting ready to come back as separates and together as an ensemble.

Savalas, best known as the lollipop-licking *Kojak,* stars in a third movie revival of his old series next month. Edwards, the surly young doctor of *Ben Casey,* has just signed a deal to bring back Casey for the first time in a made-for-TV movie that may be a pilot for a new series. And both men are coming back in February in *The Dirty Dozen: The Deadly Mission,* a sequel to 1985's *Dirty Dozen: The Next Mission.* (p. D20)

The metaphor opening would be the same, without the word like. Some comparisons read better phrased in the simile form, others fit the metaphor best.

Here are two other interesting simile openings, from two separate issues of *The New York Times Book Review.*

This review of W.M. Spackman's *A Little Decorum, For Once* was published in *The Book Review* and was written by Wendy Lesser (1985), editor of *The Threepenny Review:*

Reading "A Little Decorum, For Once" is a bit like sitting in a cafe and overhearing a rather pretentious but nonetheless riveting conversation at the next table. On one hand, you can't believe that people really talk like that. On the other, you're thrilled at having acquired this stolen bit of "real life." (p. 14)

The second is a review of Robert Ludlum's *The Bourne Supremacy.* The reviewer is playwright and novelist David Wiltse (1986).

Reading Robert Ludlum's latest thriller is a bit like watching a blacksmith forge a very long chain. The making of the first few links is interesting enough as an exercise in brute manipulation. What is lacking in finesse and artistry is made up for by lots of noise and energy. But after watching the smith link together a foot or so of chain, one perceives a certain sameness to the effort. The chief suspense is how long the man will keep at it. (p. 12)

(What a damaging review!)

Writing in the University of Texas student newspaper, *The Daily Texan,* Sean S. Price (1987) reviewed the CBS television series, "Hard Copy" using a simile beginning:

Like teenage boys peeking into a girls' locker room, *Hard Copy*'s intentions are fairly obvious.

CBS's latest stab at thoughtful drama—this time revolving around the lives of big-city crime reporters—wants very badly to be the next *Hill Street Blues* or *St. Elsewhere.*

And while its premise isn't so awful, it's difficult to see *Hard Copy,* which Channel 7 airs Sunday nights at 9 p.m., knocking off the likes of *Lou Grant* as TV Land's best rendition of what real-life journalists are like. (TV Watch section, p. 2)

You probably remember the first sentence of Tom Paine's *The Crisis Papers*. Do you recall the simile in the third sentence?

These are the times that try men's souls. The summer soldier and the sunshine patriot will in this crisis, shrink from the service of his country; but he that stands it NOW, deserves the love and thanks of man and woman. Tyranny, like hell, is not easily conquered; yet we have this consolation with us, that the harder the conflict, the more glorious the triumph. What we obtain too cheap, we esteem too lightly.

The most famous simile in America is the opening to A.J. Liebling's (1961) biography of Governor Huey Long of Louisiana, *The Earl of Louisiana*.

Southern political personalities, like sweet corn, travel badly. The lost flavor with every hundred yards away from the patch. By the time they reach New York, they are like Golden Bantam, which has been trucked up from Texas—stale and unprofitable. The consumer forgets that the corn tastes different where it grows. That, I suppose, is why for twenty-five years I underrated Huey Pierce Long. (p. 7)

Austin, Texas free lancer Deidre A. Hanley (1988) used a fine simile beginning in an article about the art of chili-cooking, which she titled "Make No Beans About Chili." Her beginning:

Like snowflakes and fingerprints, no two pots of chili are exactly alike. But for those who love chili, and there are many of them, this is the beauty of the dish. No matter how many different versions a person tries, and no matter how good a particular version is, a "chili head" can always find comfort in the belief that they could make it just a little bit better.

Chili—that delicate marriage between meat and fire—has seen its popularity ebb and flow over the years. But regardless of current fad, there always remains those for whom a steaming bowl of "son-of-a-bitch stew" is more than a meal. It is a cultural identity.

Although Boston takes pride in its chowder and Louisiana garners fame for its gumbo, Texas divides and falls over chili. Yet despite the fact that chili became the official state dish of Texas in 1977, and that chili is served on Capitol Hill every March 2 in honor of Texas Independence Day, not even Texas chili lovers can agree on what constitutes as perfect bowl of red.

My favorite simile beginning is from an article "Baseball, Hotdogs, Apple Pie and Folk Art" by Austin free lancer Annette McGivney Wysocki (1983). Her beginning:

Folk artists are like wildflowers. The most beautiful thing about them is that they are uncultivated.

Yet many of these unique wild flowers go unnoticed because they are hidden in a forest. And the crafts of many fascinating folk artists are never recognized because they are deeply buried in a community.

Pat Jasper looks for these special art forms in places where they grow; in living rooms, pool halls and school yards. She wants to discover the folk arts of Texas—that's her job.

Jasper is the Folk Arts Coordinator for the Texas Commission on the Arts, a state agency designed to service and promote the arts in Texas.

Name: Simile or metaphor beginning.

Frequency of use: Rarely seen.

Length: Varies.

Difficulty range: 7–9. Seldom easy to craft an exceptional simile or metaphor opening.

THE "FALSE" BEGINNING

"Miss April was photographed bowling"

In this opening, the writer leaves out one very important aspect to innocently direct the reader to "another time, another place." No writer would deliberately lie to an audience, but in this opening, we *suggest* a different idea than the reality, by leaving out a key element of the story.

What do you think when you read the phrase "Miss April" or "Miss November"? *Playboy*? *Penthouse*? Here is an Associated Press feature from Springfield, Massachusetts, moved on the AP wire Dec. 31, 1986:

> SPRINGFIELD, Mass. (AP)—"Miss April" was photographed bowling before spectators in wheelchairs. "Miss November" held a copy of *National Geographic* behind her spectacled nose. The centerfold wore pearls and a hospital wristband.
>
> These pinups were among the many residents of Ring Nursing homes who were photographed for a 1987 calendar.
>
> Their average age is 85 and their wrinkles are untouched, but they are popular, said nursing home president Matthew J. Leahey.
>
> Leahey said the first batch of 400 calendars was quickly snapped up by the residents at the two homes in Springfield and their families, and a second printing of 400 calendars also is going fast as other relatives hear of the project.
>
> The calendars cost about $2.50 each to produce, but are given to residents, their families and staff at no cost.
>
> "I've already given two away and now my niece wants one, too," said Nicolina Caporale, 83, of Springfield, who, as "Miss August," sports a straw cowboy hat.

Ronald B. Taylor (1987), writing for *The Los Angeles Times* service, used a long descriptive lead for an article about cowboys, which was moved across *The Times* wire service early in January.

As you begin reading this article, ask yourself: When does this take place?

As descriptive and fascinating as this beginning is, Taylor did not use a specific date in reference to when the story took place—until well into the fourth long paragraph and into the fifth. The time is now. The article appeared in some newspapers under the headline:

Little dogies
get along on
fall round-up

Sierra cattle drive races
winter across mountains

BROWN COW RAMP, Calif.—It was still dark as a dozen cowboys rode out of the forest and across the frosty meadow. Ice-bright stars glinted in the black sky and coyotes yapped and howled from a nearby ridge, signaling that dawn was not far off.

Fall was quickly turning to winter in the southern Sierra Nevada and the riders—cold faces tucked deep into the folds of their winter coats—were in a hurry. They had to be in Ramshaw Meadows by daylight to gather the Double Circle L cattle for the drive out of the mountains.

With the summer grazing season in the Inyo National Forest at an end, cattleman John Lacey's crew had to get hundreds of cows and their fat calves safely out of the high country and into the low-lying grasslands of the Owens Valley before snowstorms trapped them.

The 30-mile, four-day cattle drive—oldest, largest and longest in the state, according to the California Cattleman's Association—is a holdover from the Old West. It starts in the large meadows of the Golden Trout Wilderness at the north end of the Kern Plateau, passes over the Sierra crest and winds down through precipitous canyons, ending at the Lacey ranch near the town of Olacha, nearly 200 miles north of Los Angeles.

Because the summer range that Lacey leases from the government is in the wilderness, there are no roads. Helicopters, trucks or other modern equipment are prohibited and the Lacey cowboys, among them vounteers who jump at the chance to ride long hours, drink whiskey and tell tall tales, punch cows the old-fashioned way, on horseback. The two cow camps—log cabins and pole corrals in brown and Templeton meadows—are supplied by mule trains just as they were in the 1880s.

Up here cowboys still wear pistols, chew tobacco and drink whiskey early and late. They roll out of their bedrolls long before daylight and put in long hours gathering and herding cattle over timbered mountains and through icy streams, just as Lacey cowhands have done for 100 years.

Here is a nearly ideal false opening, in an article by Kathy Hacker (1985), moved on the Knight-Ridder news wire. Can you guess which element was left out of the story? I'll save the headline until after the opening segment, a spacebreak and two summary paragraphs after the jump:

NEW YORK—Twenty-two floors above Manhattan's modish Fashion Avenue, in a designer showroom streaked with the light of a waning sun, the transformation begins.

First, a thin layer of foundation was smoothed along the jaw, over the nose and across the forehead, followed by generous puffs of powder that floated upward in a dusty pink cloud. Each cheek got a daub of rouge and each eyelid a dramatic smudging of white shadow above dark. The lashes were coated with mascara, the mouth painted with glistening bordello-red lipstick.

Black-stockinged feet slipped into spike-heeled pumps and then stepped gingerly into the piece de resistance: a sleek, rhinestone-studded gown from the fall collection of Kenneth Bonavitacola. Wound low around the shoulders was a wide sash of white satin, with an elephantine bow at the bust and acres of bare skin above. It needed no jewelry, save a pair of over-sized pave diamond earrings from which dangled strands of pearls. All that was left now was the coif, to be slicked back at the sides, poufed voguishly on top and doused with enough spray to preserve it for eternity.

When it was done, a hush fell over the showroom. "Stunning!" murmured one observer. "Astounding!" gasped another. The rest stood transfixed, as well they might, at the thoroughly arresting sight of Kevin. Kevin in a dress.

"People may say to me, 'How dare you wear that!' " he sniffed, pirouetting before a bank of full-length mirrors, stopping mid-twirl to straighten his pantyhose and smile vampishly into the glass. "I say to them, 'How dare I not!' I happen to wear it well."

No matter how one tells it, the story of Kevin Boyce always ends up sounding like an Andy Warhol rewrite of Horatio Alger.

Misunderstood boy from Small Town U.S.A. (in this case, Upper Darby, Pa.) packs up his bags, bids Mom and Dad adieu and, with not much more than a train ticket in his pocket, heads off to the Big City to be Somebody.

Now you realize that writer Hacker omitted the model's name—and sex. The article appeared in some publications under the title and subtitle:

> Pretty Boy
> Fashion world has never seen
> anything like Kevin in a dress

Here's another similar article, by Marjorie Hyer (1987), moved on *The Washington Post* wire service. The subject: Lesley Northrup. What element of the story is missing in the beginning?

WASHINGTON—Lesley Northup wanted a baby.

Like many women of her generation, Northup, now 40, had focused all her energies first on education and professional training, then on establishing herself in her career. But the deep urge to create and nurture new life would not be denied.

She had no plans to marry. An adoption was beyond her budget. So, on three successive nights in December 1985, she inseminated herself with sperm from three different, carefully chosen donors. Fifteen-month-old Evan Arandes Northup, her soft brown hair framing a face that seems a small replica of her mother's, is the result.

Single women opting to have babies by artificial insemination, while far from commonplace, have gained increasing acceptance in today's changing sexual mores.

But Lesley Northup is a priest of the Episcopal Church, bound by ordination vows to live her life as "a wholesome example" of Christian precepts. Northup, an intense, articulate woman, believes that there is nothing in her route to parenthood to strain those vows.

And so far, leaders of her church agree. They say that her actions, although unusual, have not violated any biblical commandment or prevented her from serving as a priest.

"I have done nothing illegal or immoral in having this child," Northup said. "I cannot think what the offense might be. Adultery? None of the parties was married. Extramarital sex? No sexual act occurred."

Clearly her role as a priest was the key to the story. And that appeared for the first time in the fifth paragraph. Some newspapers carried this article below the headline "Priest finds path to motherhood."

Yet the false opening does not have to be that long to be effective. Here's a much shorter false opening, moved on the AP news wire (1985):

> NEW YORK (AP)—The U.S. Department of Agriculture's new agent at Kennedy International Airport is the no-nonsense type. Heavy-jowled, never smiling, he trudges down the line at Customs inspecting suitcases with a weary eye.
>
> Okay, he does wag his tail a lot.
>
> He is Agriculture Agent O1D, better known as Jackpot or, to close friends, just plain J.P.
>
> His job, as an agent of the USDA Animal and Plant Health Inspection Service, is to sniff out contraband food being brought into the United States from abroad. He is one of four beagles participating in a test program at airports in New York, Los Angeles, San Francisco and Houston.

And here's another shorter wire story by Mark A. Uhlig (1987) in *The New York Times,* and also published nationwide, through *The New York Times* wire service:

> NEW YORK—Sometimes a guy like Rocco Morabito just feels like hitting the road.
>
> So, about 7 a.m. Friday, the young man from Port Chester, N.Y., borrowed his mom's car, picked up his baby sister and set off down the highway.
>
> Two-and-a-half miles from his home, Rocco, 5, was pulled over by a police officer concerned that the tan station wagon—which was obeying all traffic rules—appeared to be driverless.
>
> Officer Robert Vogel caught up with Rocco's car, which was maneuvering through rush-hour traffic at about 20 mph.

Vogel said he turned on his lights and siren, "and the car pulls over to the curb, in perfect accordance with the laws of New York state."

Rocco, wearing pajamas and sneakers, and his 2-year-old sister, began to cry.

Family members told police that Rocco's mother was ill and his father was working when Rocco took the keys from his mother's purse, opened the garage door, backed out, and began his adventure.

"I told them their mommy would have to come get them," Vogel said, "but the kid says: 'My mommy can't come here, because I have the only car. I can drive. I'll go get her.' "

What headline would you write for that story? The one that caught my eye was: "Boy, 5, Puts the Pedal to the Metal, but Just Barely, in Family Car."

Although it might be rare to see a "Kevin in a dress" story, or a "Priest finds path to motherhood" story, it is less rare to see a "dog detective" or "Kid driver" article. They can often be found in local newspapers and on the wires; stories about dog detectives, swimming pool guard dogs, and kiddie drivers.

If you leave the *age* element out of the beginning of a story—you let your reader form a mental picture of "Miss April" or "Miss November." If you leave the *time* element out of the beginning of a story, you let the reader form a mental picture of the old west. If you leave the *name and sex* out of the beginning of a story, you let the reader form a mental picture of a New York high fashion model. And if you leave the *species* out of the beginning of a story—you have the "heavy-jowled, never smiling" customs inspector.

How could *you* use the false opening?

Name: False opening.

Frequency of use: Seen occasionally.

Length: Varies, from one short paragraph to several long paragraphs.

Difficulty range: 6–9. Most stories do not lend themselves to this treatment.

THE "MEMO TO" BEGINNING

"Dear Steve:"

The art of letter writing is a thing of the past—we telephone rather than write, these days—but the "open letter" or "memo to" beginning *can* be effective if you are writing opinion material, have a bylined newspaper or magazine column or are writing editorial-type "think material."

The "open letter" or "memo to" is phrased like a letter.

This can be from you as author or could be a fictional letter to a real person.

In a recent column, syndicated columnist William Raspberry addressed an "open letter" to presidential aide Pat Buchanan, suggesting how the Reagan administration might off-set the problems of the Iran arms deal. The Raspberry column began essentially like this:

Mr. Pat Buchanan,
The White House
Dear Pat;

In a different style, Martha Bayles (1986) wrote to Stephen Bochco, producer of the TV series "L.A. Law," about the show. Bayles sent a letter from "John J. Yuppie," member of the mythical law firm "UpScale, Demos, Lubricity, & Viscera." Her letter appeared in *The Wall Street Journal* on the op-ed page, under the title, "An Attorney's Complaint."

John J. Yuppie
Upscale, Demos, Lubricity & Viscera
Attorneys-at-Law
Los Angeles, California

Mr. Stephen Bochco
Bochco Independent Productions
Hollywood, California

September 14, 1992

Dear Steve;

As a young attorney about to become a partner in a prestigious firm, I simply had to write and tell you that it was an episode of your hit series "L.A. Law" that inspired me to pursue such a career. The episode was called "Sidney, the Dead-Nosed Reindeer," and it aired during the show's first season, way back in December of 1986.

What a terrific deal, I thought, just three short years in law school, and I, too, can enjoy a torrid romance with the sultry wife in a divorce case while representing the wimpy husband. I, too, can snicker at a pathetic little inventor who claims to have designed the world's first "self-wringing tea bag." I, too, can shudder at the terrible eloquence of a flamboyantly self-destructive colleague named Sidney, who blows his brains out in a courtroom. Lust, greed, humor, anguish—score above average on the law boards, I told myself, and life will overflow with rich authentic experiences.

Later in the letter to Bochco, "John J. Yuppie" writes:

The fact is, Steve, real victims are a pain. Compared with your self-wringing variety, real sufferers do not make eloquent speeches about the ironic relevance of their personal misery to larger questions of social policy (if they're black) or the meaning of existence (if they're white). Nor do they necessarily turn to their attorneys for solace. Perhaps it's my lack of pulchritude, but almost never does a really unhappy and brutalized client, like the one played by Ms. Woodard, show up at my office late at night begging for my tender embrace. I'm lucky if they'll even talk to me, much less trust me with the truth, provided, of course, that they can recognize what the truth is. (p. 15)

The letter was signed:

> Regrets from an ex-fan,
> John

Name: Memo or "open letter" beginning.
Frequency of use: Seen occasionally.
Length: Varies
Difficulty range: 3–4.

Advisory.   Often most effective with editorial material, columns, bylined material, reviews, and opinion essays.

THE "DREAM" BEGINNING

"I was dreaming I was home"

Another relatively rare beginning is the dream opening, which could be based on a figurative or literal dream. This is seen more in books than in newspaper or magazine material.

Alice's Adventures in Wonderland was a dream and was fiction. Here is a dream opening from a moving book of nonfiction, Dr. Albert Haas's 1984 autobiography, *The Doctor and the Damned:*

> I was dreaming that I was home. I was busy in the living room with Sonja and Francois, my wife and baby son, as if we had never been separated. We were preparing a party to celebrate our son's first birthday. The German occupation of France had not yet invaded our small apartment in Nice. The feelings of warmth and security were almost as palpable as the abundance of food set out on our table. It was a festive display unaffected by the shortages of wartime. Yet underneath it all drifted a vague sense of threat.
>
> The sight of Sonja holding our infant son in her arms reassured me. I wondered out loud when her sister and mother would arrive for the birthday party.
>
> There was a knock at the door. I could not move to answer it. My heart began to pound. Anxiety knotted my insides.
>
> Voices called out. They were not speaking French. I began to wake up. I fought to hold on to my illusion of reality. The impact of my dream receded slowly, leaving me too disoriented to comprehend my dreary room or the words being shouted through the door.
>
> The gutteral language crystallized into meaning: *Haftling Artz, aufstehen!*" ("Prisoner-physician, wake up!") The SS *Sanitatsdienst* wants you! There has been a work accident. Bring your instruments—you will have to operate!"

I awoke from my dream into my living nightmare. It was late November, 1944. I was a doctor in the concentration camp Gusen II. (p. 3)

Here is a fascinating "dream beginning" in an article by Howard Rosenberg (1987), moved on *The Los Angeles Times* wire service. The article appeared in The Austin (Texas) *American-Statesman* under the headline "Actress with MS still 'dreams of dancing' ":

Madlyn Rhue is dancing.

The orchestra is playing Cole Porter in an elegant, filmy sequence resembling a 1940s musical. Madlyn glides nimbly and gracefully to the music, her long legs carrying her up a flight of marble stairs to a vast mirrored ballroom romantically lit by crystal chandeliers. There she is met by her tall, tuxedoed partner. Her long, milky-white gown sparkles and her translucent sleeves billow as she's twirled by him across the polished floor. She is dancing wonderfully.

• • •

It is a dream.

Actress Madlyn Rhue has multiple sclerosis, a chronic, progressive disease of the central nervous system. These days she dances only in her dreams and in her memories.

"At the Emmys a number of years ago, they cleared the floor for Earl Holliman and me," she said. "It was Fred and Ginger. I'm a wonderful dancer."

Was a wonderful dancer.

Rhue began her show business career as a 17-year-old dancer in New York's Copacabana before moving on to the Latin Quarter and ultimately becoming a successful actress. And now, 33 years later, she is in a wheelchair, an actress with 10 movies and scores of television credits in her past, stricken with a disease for which there is no known cure.

MS hit and floored Rhue.

"I got it 10 years ago for my 40th birthday," she cracked, displaying the humor that mingles with traces of melancholy. "I was in the Broadway with my girlfriend, Suzanne (Pleshette). I turned to talk to her and suddenly I threw up, urinated and fainted.'

That was Rosenberg's beginning. He then summarized Rhue's plight in three poignant, dramatic paragraphs:

Rhue cried and cursed when told finally that she had MS. She had been one of those artists whose face was more familiar than her name; not quite a star, but a good, steadily working character actress who was in her prime.

Give or take an occasional bit role, however, an actress with MS was potentially an actress without work in an industry that, especially then, recoiled from hiring the handicapped for acting roles.

So she hid her MS, and for years only her doctor knew about her illness. "I was telling people I had a car accident," Rhue said.

This dream beginning is almost always written in the first-person; Haas's powerful opening segment of his book is typical of how dramatic such a beginning can be.

Name: The dream beginning.
Frequency of use: Rare.
Length: Varies.
Difficulty range: 9–10.

Advisory.   This beginning is a powerful and significant one; it is usually most appropriate for dramatic, confessional, or autobiographical material.

THE HISTORICAL BEGINNING

"Back in 1884, a handful of New Yorkers took a deep breath and"

You could think of this as a "remember when?" beginning, because that is what the beginning demands of the reader.

You can use this beginning to show how much different we are now, than X years ago, or how much we remained the same.

This opening reminds readers what it was like a year ago, a decade ago, or a half-century ago.

In this story about Dallas Cowboy running back Tony Dorsett, *Dallas Times Herald* staff writer Jim Dent (1986) used an historical opening to show how long Dorsett has been setting running records. The article title in *The Times Herald* was:

> Injury Probably
> to End Dorsett's
> 1,000-Yard Run

Tony Dorsett was a monster man on the Hopewell High School team in the steel country of western Pennsylvania when he last failed to rush for 1,000 yards during a full season.

Richard Nixon was President. U.S. troops were in Vietnam. The Cowboys had yet to play in their first Super Bowl.

"It was so long ago that I really don't remember it," Dorsett said Thursday as he pulled an elastic supporter over his left knee.

It was the fall of 1970 and Dorsett was a monster—a rover with no set responsibilities—on Hopewell's team. A year later, during his junior season, he would be moved to offense. Dorsett started rolling and he didn't stop.

Until the strike-shortened 1982 season, when NFL teams played only nine regular-season games, the yearly ritual was intact.

That season, he finished with 745 yards. At that pace, though, he could have gained 1,324 during a 16-game season.

Excluding the '82 season, Dorsett's 1,000-yard seasons have spanned 14 years. But the streak is almost certain to stop this season because of a knee injury that still causes him to limp.

"For a running back to have a knee injury is like having terminal cancer," Dorsett said. "It's like having cancer as far as your career is concerned. It can end it at any moment.

"There is no doubt that the knee has slowed me down quite a bit, but I'm on my way back. So I hope to finish up the season strong." (p. D1)

Here are two more historical beginnings from *The Wall Street Journal,* both interesting and appropriate to the article. The first article, by staff reporter Cynthia Sanz (1984), ran under the title:

What Stops Hearts,
Is Somewhat Sadistic
And Is 100 Years Old?

Back in 1884, a handful of New Yorkers took a deep breath and hopped on a wooden mine car affixed to a small track at Coney Island. Up the car climbed to peaks reaching four feet, then down at speeds approaching six miles an hour. Forty-five seconds later, the nation's first roller coaster pulled into its makeshift station. America never got off.

Now, in the centennial year of this quintessential cheap thrill, roller-coaster riders whiz by in far racier contraptions. High technology enables them to drop from heights of 10-story buildings, speed upside down through vertical loops at 70 mph and then hurdle through corkscrew loops backward. Big-time amusement parks are scrambling to keep their coaster state-of-the-art, in order to draw jaded riders seeking everything from heart-stopping excitement to a cure for what ails them.

Consider Janice Garza of Houston. After reading in a supermarket tabloid that coasters loosen up arthritic joints, the 59-year-old grandmother began riding Astroworld's Texas Cyclone, which features sharp curves, 60-mph speeds and a 90-foot drop that is among the steepest around. "It's hard to tell whether it works or not, because when you get off you feel wobbly," Mrs. Garza says, admitting that her doctor frowns on the "treatment." (p. 1)

The second article by staff writers Rich Jabroslovsky and James M. Perry (1984), was published under the headline:

New Question in Race:
Is Oldest U.S. President
Now Showing His Age?

WASHINGTON—When he was born, the flag that flew over the post office in his home town had 46 stars. William Howard Taft was president. And windshields had just been introduced as standard equipment on automobiles.

At the age of 73, Ronald Reagan is the oldest president this nation ever had.

And he is approaching what many gerontologists say is an important milestone in the aging process. Lawrence Klein, a professor of medicine at Georgetown and Johns Hopkins Universities, explains that in layman's terms, Mr. Reagan is now in the "young–old" bracket. That takes in a group between 65 and 75. Soon, though, says Dr. Klein, the president will edge into the "old–old" bracket.

Until Sunday night's debate, age hadn't been much of an issue in the election campaign. That may now be changing. The president's rambling responses and occasional apparent confusion injected an unpredictable new element into the race.

Eugene Jennings, a management expert at Michigan State University, who backed Mr. Reagan in 1980 says, "I am very concerned, as a psychologist, about his inability to think on his feet, the disjointedness of his sentences and his use of the security blanket of redundancy. . . . I'd be concerned to put him in a corporate presidency. I'd be all the more concerned to put him into the U.S. president." (p. 1)

Name: Historical beginning.

Frequency of use: Seen occasionally.

Length: Varies with subject.

Difficulty range: 3–4. Relatively easy to construct.

Advisory.   If you use an historical opening or a diary form opening, *check and re-check your math.* Make sure all numbers add up correctly. There is no more obvious mistake in an article than a mathematical error. *Never assume an editor will check your numbers for you.*

THE ASTONISHING BEGINNING

"Jasper Maskelyne was drinking a glass of razor blades when the war began"

Once in months or years, a writer has material so powerful it is a natural to begin with an astonishing statement. This might be called a "Ripley's Believe It or Not" opening.

What do you think of this opening sentence:

Jasper Maskelyne was drinking a glass of razor blades when the war began.

Wouldn't that pull you into the story?

That's the beginning of David Fisher's 1983 book, *The War Magician,* a book I could not put down from the opening sentence. It's a biography of

Maskelyne, an English music hall magician, drafted in the British Army to trick the Germans with *magic.*

Here are author David Fisher's first two paragraphs:

> Jasper Maskelyne was drinking a glass of razor blades when the war began. It was an old trick, first made popular by his grandfather, the legendary John Nevil Maskelyne, and often performed by his father, Nevil Maskelyne, but it always delighted the audience. As he began withdrawing from his mouth the six sharp blades, conveniently knotted to a cotton string like tiny steel sheets on a clothesline, he first noticed the young army captain moving anxiously down the center aisle. He was careful not to stare at the officer, lest he divert attention to him, but still managed to watch him scanning the rows. The captain finally stopped near the front and leaned over a handsome woman to whisper something to a colonel. By the time Jasper had discovered the live rose sprouting from the stageboards, and picked it, the colonel was walking briskly out of the theater. He did not look back.
>
> Jasper sniffed the scarlet flower, briefly luxuriating in its fragrance, then tossed it into the air. Suddenly, it burst into smoke and vanished. The audience cheered this trick, and he bowed and accepted their applause, but even as he did he thought of the two soldiers and realized it was peace that had disappeared. (p. 9)

Perhaps magic and magicians *deserve* this writing technique. Another astonishing opening was used by Ricky Jay (1986), in a chapter in his book, *Learned Pigs & Fireproof Women.* Another magician, James Randi (1986) wrote, in an issue of *The New York Times Book Review,* that the book was about "the most satisfying array of oddities, marvels and novelties that has been gathered together in a blue moon," consisting of "*very* strange folk who attracted the kind of curiosity reserved for unique, bizarre and incredible phenomena" (p. 1).

Here is Jay's beginning in a chapter titled "A Few Words About Death and Show Biz":

> Washington Irving Bishop was born in 1856; he died in 1873, 1881, and 1889. His act was peculiar. His habits were peculiar. His death was *most* peculiar. (p. 157)

James Randi, in *The Times Book Review* observed, "Who can resist that opening?"

Who indeed.

But that technique is not limited to magic—it has been used successfully in medical writing as well. Here is the beginning segment to Oliver Sacks' (1986) book *The Man Who Mistook His Wife for a Hat and Other Clinical Tales:*

> Dr. P. was a musician of distinction, well-known for many years as a singer, and then, at the local School of Music, as a teacher. It was here, in relation

to his students, that certain strange problems were first observed. Sometimes a student would present himself, and Dr. P. would not recognise him; or, specifically, would not recognise his face. The moment the student spoke, he would be recognised by his voice. Such incidents multiplied, causing embarrassment, perplexity, fear—and, sometimes, comedy. For not only did Dr. P. increasingly fail to see faces, but he saw faces when there were no faces to see: genially Magoo-like, when in the street he might pat the heads of water hydrants and parking meters, taking them to be the heads of children; he would amiably address carved knobs on the furniture and be astonished when they did not reply. At first these odd mistakes were laughed off as jokes, not least by Dr. P. himself. Had he not always had a quirky sense of humour and been given to Zen-like paradoxes and jests? His musical powers were as dazzling as ever; he did not feel ill—he never felt better; and the mistakes were so ludicrous— and so ingenious—that they could hardly be serious or betoken anything serious. The notion of there being 'something the matter' did not emerge until some three years later, when diabetes developed. Well aware that diabetes could affect his eyes, Dr. P consulted an opthalmologist, who took a careful history and examined his eyes closely. 'There's nothing the matter with your eyes,' the doctor concluded. 'But there is trouble with the visual parts of your brain. You don't need my help, you must see a neurologist.' And so, as a result of this referral, Dr. P. came to me. (p. 8)

The first sentence of the autobiography *My Father and Myself,* by J.R. Ackerley (1969) begins: "I was born in 1896 and my parents were married in 1919" (p. 11). And although this is clearly an "I" form beginning, I found it so astonishing that I list it in this category. "The writer of these words, the first sentence of this memoir, was a shy homosexual, his father a hard-drinking womanizer. In reconstructing his private life, the author and editor J.R. Ackerley produced 'a classic of autobiographical literature,' " *The New York Times Book Review* said, in the Jan. 31, 1988 issue. (p. 34)

Finally, an ingenuous beginning to an early profile of James Thurber, written by Arthur Millier and titled "Melancholy Doodler," was published in *The Los Angeles Times Sunday Magazine* July 2, 1939. Millier wrote:

As I shook hands with James Thurber, I looked him straight in the eye and said that I understood he was quite, quite mad.

Well, maybe I didn't exactly say it out loud. Maybe what I really said was "Where and when were you born?" But so deft a psychologist as Thurber couldn't have missed the implication.

"Columbusohioeighteenninetyfour," he replied at more than Winchell speed. "That makes me forty-four. A terrible age. It scares me because there's only one way out—through the fifties. Heh heh. And I'm not mad." (p. 6)

And on a separate page, before Chapter One in his novel *The Boys of Winter,* Wilfrid Sheed offers the reader this Author's Note:

Great literature is, of course, timeless.
This novel is set in 1978.

Name: Astonishing beginning.
Frequency of use: Rare.
Length: Varies.
Difficulty range: 9–10. Nearly impossible to use with "common" material.

THE "BIOGRAPHICAL CAPSULE" BEGINNING

"He was a combination of"

The biographical capsule is neither simply an anecdote about a personality, nor is it just a quotation from or about that personality.

Rather, it is a biographical *collage.*

One of the definitions of *collage* in *Webster's Third International Dictionary* is: "an assembly of diverse fragments."

This assembly of diverse fragments presented at the beginning of a profile or biography should capture the reader's interest: The collage should show the breadth, depth, scope, versatility, and accomplishments of the personality.

Just as the Mosaic opening (p. 61) is a *collage of details,* the biographical capsule is a *collage of personality.*

Here are three examples of biographical capsule beginnings. They all happen to be from recent books, but the technique could certainly work in shorter nonfiction as well. The title of the book and the author's names are listed after the citation:

> Frederick Lewis Allen's best-selling histories imprinted upon the minds of millions of Americans a captivating and indelible image of their own yesterdays. His engaging style of writing made the past enjoyable as well as informative not only for Americans but for readers of his books in Great Britain, Italy, Japan, and the Soviet Union. His assessment of the 1920s became a point of departure for later historians, and his history of that period, *Only Yesterday,* has been declared a "classic." Allen, however, considered history to be no more than a secondary interest. He wrote his books by squeezing time out of evenings, weekends, vacations, and occasional leaves of absence from his full-time work.
>
> First and foremost Allen was an editor. For thirty-one years, twelve of them as editor in chief, he was employed by *Harper's Magazine,* where he dealt with many of America's foremost writers and confronted the nation's most critical problems. His life provides other vistas, too, for seeing the first half of the twentieth century in America. He was Allen the pioneer publicist, shaping public

opinion for the government during World War I and later establishing Harvard's first publicity office; Allen the humorist whose sketches appeared consistently in the nation's leading magazines; Allen the collaborator who teamed with Agnes Rogers Allen in producing pictorial history books and television scripts; Allen the man of affairs, two-term Harvard overseer, trustee of the Ford Foundation, and director of the Foreign Policy Association; Allen the family man who overcame personal tragedy; and Allen the disciplined child of Puritan New England who inherited a high sense of purpose.

In many ways Frederick Lewis Allen represents a bridge between the elitist, genteel tradition of nineteenth-century society and the casual, mobile scene that developed at mid-twentieth century. He found himself no less at home in the modern society of the 1950s than he did in the closely knit cultural and social center of Boston at the turn of the century. (pp. 1–2)

The Man of Only Yesterday:
Frederick Lewis Allen
by Darwin Payne

When James Thurber returned to Columbus in 1953 to receive the Ohioana Sesquicentennial Medal, he thanked his hosts and said, "It is a great moment for an Ohio writer living far from home when he realizes that he has not been forgotten by the state he can't forget." And he added that his books "prove that I am never very far from Ohio in my thoughts, and that the clocks that strike in my dreams are the clocks of Columbus."

He was not indulging in merely sentimental rhetoric. Although he lived more than half of his life in the East and became one of the makers and shapers of *The New Yorker,* Columbus and the Thurber family pattern of old-fashioned domesticity and eccentric behavior were the primary forces in shaping his imagination. More than most writers, he depended upon his memory of personal experiences for his artistic materials, and Columbus manners, Columbus mores, and Columbus values remained an essential part of his mind and personality. He returned time and again to the city of his birth, visiting his mother and his brothers, giving out interviews, making speeches, and reminiscing affectionately about people and events in the days gone by. "I have always waved banners and blown horns for good old Columbus town. . . . and such readers as I have collected through the years are all aware of where I was born and brought up, and they know that half of my books could not have been written if it had not been for the city of my birth," he wrote in 1952. On the other hand, it is only one of the paradoxes of his complex character that he was a Columbus product who read Henry James and James Joyce, a parodist and humorist who appealed to a highbrow audience, a cosmopolitan equally at home in London, Paris, Bermuda, and New York. He was a combination of old-fashioned Middle Western values and intellectual culture, and it is the tension between these forces which underlies much of the comedy and some, at least, of the melancholy and nostalgia in his work. (pp. 3–4)

The Clocks of Columbus:
The Literary Career of James Thurber
by Charles S. Holmes

Walter Lippmann began his career in the halcyon days before the First World War, when human progress seemed unlimited and inevitable, when poets danced in the squares and science promised a life of leisure and abundance for all. He ended it with the trauma of Vietnam, the shame of Watergate, and rioters running through the streets. His career spanned a century, a century during which the American empire was born, matured, and began to founder, a time that some have called, first boastfully, then wistfully, the American Century.

As a small boy in the 1890s, Walter Lippmann shook hands with President McKinley, was formally presented to Admiral Dewey, and rapturously cheered Theodore Roosevelt on his return from San Juan Hill. He studied at Harvard with Santayana, took tea with William James, worked as a legman with Lincoln Steffens, debated socialism with Bernard Shaw and H.G. Wells, was in Belgium when the Germans invaded and at the House of Commons when Britain declared war in 1914. For a time he worshipped Theodore Roosevelt, and when he was twenty-five TR pronounced him to be the "most brilliant young man of his age in all the United States." He was one of the founders of the *New Republic* and among the "movers and shakers" who sounded the trumpet for a cultural and social revolution in America before the First World War. He became the *eminence grise* to Woodrow Wilson's own alter ego, Colonel House, and was a key member of the secret organization that produced the territorial part of the Fourteen Points. (p. xiii)

Walter Lippmann and the American Century
by Ronald Steel

Name: Biographical capsule beginning.

Frequency of use: Seen occasionally.

Length: Varies.

Difficulty range: 7–10.

THE MOSAIC BEGINNING

"Cannery Row . . . is a poem, a stink, a grating noise, a quality of light"

On rare occasions, the writer may "flood" the reader with impressions, bits, pieces, fragments, *shards* of description, facts, bits, quotes, and notes, and eventually let the reader piece all these together into one unified whole.

This is not only difficult but risky—because the writer may lose the reader before the point of the whole beginning is reached.

The mosaic beginning must not only be *reasonably* clear, it, like all other beginnings, must come to a conclusion that is obvious to the reader.

This is essentially a gigantic summary–descriptive opening, an Irish stew of details, swirled together for the reader.

An example? Here is the first paragraph from John Steinbeck's classic *Cannery Row:*

> Cannery Row in Monterey in California is a poem, a stink, a grating noise, a quality of light, a tone, a habit, a nostalgia, a dream. Cannery Row is the gathered and scattered, tin and iron and rust and splintered wood, chipped pavement and weedy lots and junk heaps, sardine canneries of corrugated iron, honky tonks, restaurants and whore houses and little crowded groceries, and laboratories and flophouses. Its inhabitants are, as the man once said, "whores, pimps, gamblers and sons of bitches," by which he meant Everybody. Had the man looked through another peephole he might have said "Saints and angels and martyrs and holy men," and he would have meant the same thing. (p. 1)

Here is another mosaic beginning, from an article in an issue of *Harvard* magazine. The article was written by Walter Schenkman (1981) and titled:

VITA

Johann Mattheson

Versatile musician: 1681–1764

Few musicians can claim to have engaged in as many diverse activities as Johann Mattheson. A contemporary of Bach and Handel, he is described in musical biographies as a "linguist, lawyer, harpsichordist and organist, vocalist, composer and prolific author." One should include "translator," too: Defoe's *Moll Flanders,* Richardson's *Pamela,* and selections from the Spectator, along with countless tracts of the most varied sort translated from French, Italian, and Latin, were first presented to German readers through his effort.

Mattheson also served in an official capacity as secretary to the British legation in Hamburg. There he had occasion to practice the arts and forms of diplomacy, and took credit for the signing and sealing of at least one herring treaty. In pursuits of a more private nature he demonstrated a fine business acumen, turning a profit when he edited and published a musical journal (presumably the first in Germany); and he displayed remarkable competence as carpenter and mason when he "substituted one form of composition for another" and built his own home—as well as several to rent.

This unusual figure has left us a detailed and "amusingly egotistical" (to quote *Grove's*) account of his exploits. Born in Hamburg three hundred years ago, on September 28, 1681, he was early enrolled in that city's famous Johannisschule, where he studied Latin, Greek and rhetoric. Musical training, begun at age seven, included private instruction in the keyboard, violin, viola de gamba, flute, oboe, voice, and composition. As he developed in physical stature, dancing, fencing, and riding were added to the curriculum.

In 1690, when he was nine, the rare quality of Mattheson's soprano voice earned him an invitation to sing in the Hamburg Opera; there he was to remain for the next fifteen years. Towards the end of this period (as he modestly informs us), he sang practically nothing but leading roles, "to the universal approval and grand acclaim of the spectators." (p. 37)

This beginning is not only elegant when used correctly, but involving. It is also relatively rare and difficult to pull off.

If this—and some other beginnings in this book are difficult and rare—why list them at all?

This might be the most appropriate beginning for the next story you write. And you should know it exists and that you can use it.

Name: Mosaic beginning.

Frequency of use: Relatively rare.

Length: Varies with material.

Difficulty range: 9–10. Relatively difficult form to use.

THE COMBINATION BEGINNING

"You're the doctor . . . do you let him go?"

The summary beginning, the quotation and description, the "big play" and the question beginning—and all the rest—are all appropriate beginnings for all manner of nonfiction *and* fictional beginnings. Yet in many cases, the beginning can be enhanced by *combining elements* of two or even more identifiable techniques.

These are only samples:

- A descriptive beginning could lead to an "I" form statement by the author about the scene being shown to the reader ("I think this is the most beautiful area of the country in the autumn because. . . ."):
- A problem or paradox beginning could lead to a question, as a second-person "you" phrase ("What do you think of problem XYZ?") or a regular question ("Is A or B the right way to solve this dilemma?");
- A summary beginning could lead to a significant quotation by a principal subject of the article;
- An anecdotal beginning could lead to a question ("Did Jones do the right thing in that episode?").

In fact, it is often the case that the writer will instinctively realize that a *combination of styles* is most appropriate for the subject.

Here is a combination of the dramatic second-person "you" beginning that leads to two questions. This is the opening of an article "Fateful Decisions on Treating AIDS," by Ezra Bowen (1987) (reported by B.J. Phillips in *Time*'s Paris Bureau, with other bureaus) in the February 2 issue of *Time*.

You're the doctor, and the patient is dying from AIDS. A new drug called azidothymidine (AZT) might temporarily suppress the virus and prolong his life. But you hesitate: AZT may do nothing more for his manifestations of the disease. It could even hasten death. And prescribing the drug could bring malpractice suits, since AZT has so far worked only on AIDS sufferers with symptoms different from this patient's.

Do you let him go? Or do you risk everything on the chance of helping him? These questions took on a new urgency last week when. . . . (p. 62)

Here is the beginning from Robert Penn Warren's classic novel, *All the King's Men*; this segment is about half of the first paragraph of the book:

To get there you follow Highway 58, going northeast out of the city, and it is a good highway and new. Or was new, that day we went up it. You look up the highway and it is straight for miles, coming at you, with the black line down the center coming at and at you, black and silk and tarry-shining against the white of the slab, and the heat dazzles up from the white slab so that only the black line is clear, coming at you with the whine of the tires, and if you don't quit staring at that line and don't take a few deep breaths and slap yourself hard on the back of the neck you'll hypnotize yourself and you'll come to just at the moment when the right front wheel hooks over into the black dirt shoulder off the slab, and you'll try to jerk her back on but you can't because the slab is high like a curb, and maybe you'll try to reach to turn off the ignition just as she starts the dive. But you won't make it, of course.

This narrative is almost cinematic in its vividness. It is combined dramatically with the second-person "you." Notice how many times Warren repeated "you" (or "yourself"). I count 14 uses of *you* or *yourself* in that segment.

Here is a combination beginning from an article about "The Original Christmas Store" in Houston, Texas. It was written by Doris Laird Schleuse. It combines the second-person "you" with detailed description, evoking a child's sense of wonder while walking through the doors into this Christmas wonderland:

When you walk through the doors of an original Christmas Store, your senses are bombarded. Your eyes switch to wide-angle focus. First, you see the lights. More than 90,000 tiny, bright, white lights. And they are everywhere. There are the more traditional lights, too, plus some that twinkle, some that burble and gurgle.

Blink.

You'll probably notice the animation next. Kids always do. Over against the wall, there's a mini-mountain, inhabited by about 50 furry creatures. They're all moving. They run movie projectors, jump rope, go fishing, hang out wash, play tug-a-war, cook, dance, bounce on a see-saw and seem to have a high ole time. The scene is for sale at $75,000.

Right in the middle is a carousel. Six life-size horses are moving up, down, around with the music, all under a 12-foot diameter celestial dome. Their journey is reflected in the mirrored ceiling. Price tag: $100,000.

And then there're the trees. About a hundred decorated Christmas trees. Two to 20 feet tall. All colors. And each one is a different theme. There's the Texas tree, with stars and boots and cactus and dough-bread football players. And olde-fashioned tree, with gingerbread men, bubble lights, lace, popcorn balls, icicles and an angel at the tip top. Or one for the "decorator," with mauve and dove grey satin ball and silk flowers.

Close your eyes for a second. Listen. The sounds of Christmas carols come over the speaker system. Someone is jangling sleigh bells. Music boxes tinkle. Moving toys whirl and whistle. Birds chirp. It all blends with the babble of voices and the squeals and sighs.

Your nose wasn't neglected. The scent of fresh pine is dispensed via aerosol can.

And then there's the merchandise. If it has anything to do with the holiday season, it will be in an Original Christmas Store. In all, there are more than 100,000 items in each store. Even more mind boggling: there are more than 20,000 different items in each store.

The Original Christmas Stores are not your ordinary "trim-a-tree" operations. The prices start at 29 cents and top out at $150,000. Each season, which runs from early September through mid-January, nearly a million folks troop through the doors. The average store is less than 20,000 square feet.

They have been called "the most beautiful stores in the world."

In her book *Every Night at Five,* Susan Stamberg, host of the National Public Radio show, *All Things Considered,* wrote:

This is a chance to read radio. All of the pieces have been edited for print. But converting radio into print has its limitations. You lose the laughs, for one thing. And there have been lots of them. You lose the silences too—the long, revealing pauses for thought or mutual understanding or embarrassment that built tension against the expectation of constant sound. The music of the voices can't be read, nor the music of bands, kazoos, synthesizers. By definition, the purest radio pieces don't translate into type. But you can tune in every night to hear them. (p. ix)

But *some* exceptional radio scripts are purely literary. The best radio material could be read "blind" and readers would not know they are reading a radio script. Here is one of Edward R. Murrow's broadcasts from a rooftop in London, during World War Two, from his book *This Is London.* Note the combination of the personal eyewitness "I" and the descriptive details. Murrow's script let *you* visualize London, just as it let his listeners see what he saw during the London blitz:

At the moment everything is quiet. For reasons of national as well as personal security I'm unable to tell you the exact location from which I'm speaking. Off to my left, far away in the distance, I can see just that faint-red, angry snap of antiaircraft bursts against the steel-blue sky, but the guns are so far away that it's impossible to hear them fro this location. About five minutes ago the guns in the immediate vicinity were working. I can look across just at a building not far away and see something that looks like a flash of white paint down the side, and I know from daylight observation that about a quarter of that building has disappeared—hit by a bomb the other night. Streets fan out in all directions from here, and down on one street I can see a single red light and just faintly the outline of a sign standing in the middle of the street. And again I know what that sign says, because I saw it this afternoon. It says DANGER—UNEXPLODED BOMB. Off to my left still I can see just that red snap of the antiaircraft fire.

I was up here earlier this afternoon and looking out over these housetops, looking all the way to the dome of St. Paul's. I saw many flags flying from staffs. No one ordered these people to put out the flag. They simply feel like flying the Union Jack above their roof. No one told them to do it, and no flag up there was white. I can see one or two of them just stirring very faintly in the breeze now. You may be able to hear the sounds of guns off in the distance very faintly, like someone kicking a tub. Now they're silent. Four searchlights reach up, disappear in the light of a three-quarter moon. I should say at the moment there are probably three aircraft in the vicinity of London, as one can tell by the movements of the lights and the flash of the antiaircraft guns. But at the moment in the central area everything is quiet. More searchlights spring up over on my right. I think probably in a minute we shall have the sounds of guns in the immediate vicinity. The lights are swinging over in this general direction now. You'll hear two explosions. There they are! That was the explosion overhead, not the guns themselves. I should think in a few minutes there may be a bit of shrapnel around here. Coming in—moving a little closer all the while. The plane's still very high. Earlier this evening we could hear occasional . . . again those were explosions overhead. Earlier this evening we heard a number of bombs go sliding and slithering across to fall several blocks away. Just overhead now the burst of the antiaircraft fire. Still the near-by guns are not working. The searchlights now are feeling almost directly overhead. Now you'll hear two bursts a little nearer in a moment. There they are! That hard, stony sound. (pp. 179–180)

In *The Austin American-Statesman* November 17, 1984, Thor Hansen uses a combination, a descriptive beginning, "false" beginning, and the "you" beginning to paint a vivid picture of the mists of prehistoric time in an area now known as McKinney Falls State Park, southwest of Austin, Texas. His article was headlined "Volcano shores up history, beauty at park."

His beginning:

Imagine yourself on a small tropical island. Warm-water surf crashes on a white sand beach. A small black hill sits peacefully in the center of the island, surrounded by a clear lagoon.

There is something odd about this paradise. The shells on the limestone sand are large and unfamiliar and there are no birds on the shore. Something that looks like the Loch Ness monster pokes its head out of the water and is eyeing you curiously.

But before Nessies' gaze can change to something more sinister, a violent tremor knocks you to your knees, followed by an earsplitting explosion. The peaceful little hill becomes a malevolent volcano, spewing dense lead-gray clouds of hot ash and noxious fumes.

Great Mounds of ash and debris shake loose from the sides of the hill and slide down the slope crashing and steaming into the lagoon.

The place is McKinney Falls Park. it is more than a pretty state park; it is a textbook of earth history. (TV Watch section, p. 4)

My all-time favorite beginning is the three-paragraph introduction that John Steinbeck used to "set the stage" for *Cannery Row*. The first paragraph of it was cited previously. Here are all three paragraphs, with inserts showing what techniques he uses in combination to capture the reader's attention an draw the reader into his novel:

Cannery Row in Monterey, California is a poem, a stink, a grating noise, a quality of light, a tone, a habit, a nostalgia, a dream. Cannery Row is the gathered and scattered, tin and iron and rust and splintered wood, chipped pavement and weedy lots and junk heaps, sardine canneries of corrugated iron, honky tonks, restaurants and whore houses, and little crowded groceries, and laboratories and flophouses. Its inhabitants are, as the man once said, "whores, pimps, gamblers, and sons of bitches," by which he meant Everybody. Had the man looked through another peephole he might have said, "Saints and angels and martyrs and holy men," and he would have meant the same thing. (p. 1)

The first paragraph is a classic mosaic paragraph, full of details, followed by a double metaphor: "Its inhabitants are 'whores, pimps . . .' " or " 'Saints and angels . . .' "

In the morning when the sardine fleet has made a catch, the purse-seiners waddle heavily into the bay blowing their whistles. The deep-laden boats pull in against the coast where the canneries dip their tails into the bay. The figure is advisedly chosen, for if the canneries dipped their mouths into the bay the canned sardines which emerge from the other end would be metaphorically, at least, even more horrifying. Then cannery whistles scream and all over the town men and women scramble into their clothes and come running down to the Row to go to work. Then shining cars bring the upper class down: superintendents, accountants, owners who disappear into offices. Then from the town pour Wops and Chinamen and Polaks, men and women in trousers and rubber coats and oilcloth aprons. They come running to clean and cut and pack and cook and can the fish. The whole street rumbles and groans and screams and rattles while the silver rivers of fish pour in out of the boats and the boats rise higher and higher in the water until they are empty. The canneries rumble and rattle and squeak until the last fish is cleaned and cut and cooked and canned and then the whistles scream again and the dripping, smelly, tired Wops and Chinamen and Polaks, men and women, straggle out and droop their ways up the hill into the town and Cannery Row becomes itself again—quiet and magical. Its normal life returns. The bums who retired in disgust under the black cypress tree come out to sit on the rusty pipes in the vacant lot. The girls from Dora's emerge for a bit of sun if there is any. Doc strolls from the Western Biological Laboratory and crosses the street to Lee Chong's grocery for two quarts of beer. Henri the painter noses like an Airdale through the junk in the grassgrown lot for some part or piece of wood or metal he needs for the boat he is building. Then the darkness edges in and the street light come son in front of Dora's—the lamp which makes perpetual moonlight in Cannery Row. Callers arrive at Western Biological to see Doc, and he crosses the street to Lee Chong's for five quarts of beer. (p. 1)

The second paragraph is a narrative paragraph—full of action.

How can the poem and the stink and the grating noise—the quality of light, the tone, the habit and the dream—be set down alive? When you collect marine animals there are certain flat worms so delicate that they are almost impossible to capture whole, for they break and tatter to the touch. You must let them ooze and crawl of their own onto a knife blade and then lift them gently into your bottle of sea water. And perhaps that might be the way to write this book—to open the page and let the stories crawl in by themselves. (p. 3)

The last paragraph begins with a question, adds the second-person "you" ("When you collect . . .") and follows with a simile: "This book is like delicate ocean creatures. . . ."

That's what Steinbeck's introduction to *Cannery Row* teaches us—use the techniques that work. If you have an ideal beginning that fits one category, fine. If you have an ideal beginning that includes two different forms, use it. If three beginning paragraphs contain three (or more) different techniques, using those different techniques in combination is also appropriate.

The rest of your story should follow naturally from the beginning.

THE UNCONVENTIONAL BEGINNING

"Too late now"

It is sometimes possible to write a perfectly fascinating—and appropriate beginning—which does not seem to fit any of these categories (or any you might establish).

If that happens, and if the beginning does suit the story, use it. No matter whether you can name the type of beginning or not.

Here is the beginning of a story by Leigh Montville (1987), filed on the KNT News Service wire. This ran in some newspapers under the title:

Wonderful show to remember:
the cup and land down under

FREMANTLE, Australia—Never did ask some of those sailors on the Stars & Stripes crew about their peeling faces. Three of four of those guys looked as if they continually were burning off old layers of skin and building new ones. Is this way the way they live all the time, 365 days a year, their faces falling off? Never did ask.

Too late now.

Never did have that private conversation with Dennis Conner. Never saw him—except when he was sailing the boat—with fewer than 50 people around him. Would like to have seen what lies behind that superficial exterior he wears like a cheap set of aluminum siding. Is he a good guy? Bad guy? Would like to have seen him in a relaxed surrounding.

Too late now.

Did travel to Cottlesoe Beach, where topless women lay in the sun. Found the place shameful, degenerate, disgusting. Went back next day to make sure how shameful, degenerate and disgusting the sight was. No snap judgment. Should have returned five and six and seven times more for best possible verification.

Too late now.

Had clicked into yacht-talk by the fourth race. Was talking about jibs and jibes and port and starboard and spinnakers and plastic riblets and lead keels. Finally had purged football-talk, basketball-talk and questions about whether Rich Gedman was looking for too much money. Was yacht-talk guy. Woke up in morning, looked to see which way wind was blowing to start day. Started today that way. Saw wind was heavy. Ready to talk some yacht-talk.

Too late now.

Montville has four more large paragraphs of details, with *Too late now* after each. Except the last paragraph. The article just stops. But you know what?—I'd guess almost every careful reader, enjoying Montville's refrain, said *Too late now* to themselves, at the end of the article.

I did.

Name: Unorthodox beginning.

Frequency of use: Rare.

Length: Varies.

Difficulty range: Limited only by the writer's imagination.

INSTANT CHECKLIST FOR BEGINNINGS

If you are beginning work on an article and cannot quite find the right beginning, read through this checklist. Although this may not be perfect for you, this list offers *generally appropriate* beginnings for various categories of articles.

Are you writing an article about yourself?
Consider:
- The first-person "I" beginning;
- The anecdotal beginning;
- The narrative beginning;
- The summary beginning;
- The quotation beginning;
- Other appropriate beginnings, or combinations of beginnings.

Are you writing an article about another person?
Consider:
- The anecdotal beginning;
- The descriptive beginning;
- The narrative beginning;
- The quotation beginning;
- The biographical capsule beginning;
- The comparison or contrast beginning;
- Other appropriate beginnings, or combinations of beginnings.

Are you writing an article about an event?
Consider:
- The descriptive beginning;
- The narrative beginning;
- The anecdote beginning;
- The first-person beginning;
- The summary beginning;
- Other appropriate beginnings, or combinations of beginnings.

Are you writing about a trend or problem in society?
Consider:
- The historical beginning;
- The summary beginning;
- The statement beginning;
- The quotation beginning;
- The question beginning;
- The anecdote beginning;
- Other appropriate beginnings, or combinations of beginnings.

Are you writing an editorial or an essay?
Consider:

- The statement beginning;
- The problem or paradox beginning;
- The summary beginning;
- The quotation beginning;
- The question beginning;
- Other appropriate beginnings, of combinations of beginnings.

Are you writing an article that will largely describe a location or scene?
Consider
- The descriptive beginning;
- The summary beginning;
- The mosaic beginning;
- The simile or metaphor beginning;
- Other appropriate beginnings, or combinations of beginnings.

Are you writing "self-help," "do-it-yourself," instructional, or educational material?
Consider:
- The second-person "you" beginning;
- The first-person "I" beginning;
- The summary beginning;
- The anecdote beginning;
- The quotation beginning;
- The question beginning;
- Other appropriate beginnings, or combinations of beginnings.

Are you writing psychological, religious, or motivational material?
Consider:
- The second-person "you" beginning;
- The problem or paradox beginning;
- The quotation beginning;
- The first-person "I" beginning;
- The question beginning;
- The anecdote beginning;
- The multiple example beginning;
- Other appropriate beginnings, or combinations of beginnings.

Are you writing a book review, film review, or dramatic review?
Consider:
- The summary beginning;

- The quotation beginning;
- The first-person "I" beginning;
- The second-person "you" beginning;
- The question beginning;
- Other appropriate beginnings, or combinations of beginnings.

Are you writing a sports story?
Consider:
- The summary beginning;
- The narrative ("big play") beginning;
- The front-page news beginning with the name-prominent alternative beginning;
- The quotation beginning;
- Other appropriate beginnings, or combinations of beginnings.

Are you writing a historical article?
Consider:
- The historical beginning;
- The descriptive beginning;
- The anecdote beginning;
- The quotation beginning;
- The statement beginning;
- Other appropriate beginnings, or combinations of beginnings.

Middles:
Moving Through the Article

In a section "Writing the First Draft" in *The Random House Handbook,* Frederick Crews (1980) wrote:

> Some people can write only after dark; others, only before breakfast; still others can't sit down, or need to have a radio blaring, or can write for two hours a day and not a minute more. How you manage is your affair. Maybe you should state with a later paragraph if the introductory one looks forbidding. If you are worried about losing inspiration in the middle of a sentence, you can use a private shorthand, keeping your mind on the continuity of thoughts instead of on the words. Instead of writing, you may find it easier to talk into a tape recorder and then transcribe the better parts. Whether you write or dictate, don't be afraid to include too much, and don't be embarrassed by minor imperfections. What matters is that you get the draft finished—and that you understand how much more work remains to be done afterward.
>
> Nothing is more normal than a feeling of reluctance and anxiety during the writing of a first draft. Those first few paragraphs are likely to prove especially troublesome. Have on hand ample notes, a fully developed thesis statement and an outline that looks—at least for now—logical and efficient. These are your safe passes into that scary realm, the Not Yet Written. Knowing (from your thesis statement) that you have a clear and interesting point to make, and knowing from your outline that the paragraph you are struggling with now belongs in an ordered sequence, you can talk back to that little demon who keeps saying, *You're stuck, you're stuck, you're stuck. . . .* (p. 75)

A short piece of writing is often easier than a long one; the writer sits down, begins at the beginning, and does not stop until the end, no matter how long the short piece may take.

In a long, complicated article, however, the writer may encounter 3 or 4 or as many as 10 subsections. Trying to tie all these subsections (the lead, the middle portions, the end) together involves the use of transitions. Most writers do not have much trouble with transition inside the subsection that may be the only one, two, or three pages long: The problem lies in bridging the gap between one section and another. Here are six types of transitions that help this jump from subtopic to subtopic.

- The Spacebreak: This is a physical separation of text on the page (or on a word processor screen). If you are typing doublespaced copy, when you need a "spacebreak" transition, jump six lines. The "air" or white on the page will indicate to the reader that a different topic is upcoming. Many writers will use two or three asterisks in the middle of the spacebreak to indicate to editors and readers that the jump was deliberate. This is an example of how the spacebreak looks on the page:

"XXXXXXXXXX. XXXXXXXXXXXX. XXXXXXXXXXX."

*   *   *

"XXXXXXXXXXXXXXXXX. XXXXXXXXXXXXXXXXXX."

Advisory.   This technique should be used while writing for publications that regularly employ this device. Most magazines use the spacebreak technique; many newspapers do not.

- The Spacebreak with a "Pull Out": The writer may wish to use a quotation from *later in the story* in the spacebreak. This is sometimes called a "take-out" or "pull-out" because the quote is *taken out* of the story and highlighted in the spacebreak. It still remains later in the text, however. The use of the quote as a subhead in the spacebreak indicates the same quote upcoming in the text is a significant one:

    "XXXXXXXXXX. XXXXXXXXXXXX. XXXXXXXXXXX."
XXXXXXXXXXXXXXXXXXXXXXXXXXXXXXXXX."
    "This is the best experience I have ever had."
    "XXXXXXXXXX. XXXXXXXXXXXX. XXXXXXXXXXX."
XXXXXXXXXXXXX. XXXXXXXXXXXX. XXXXXXXXX
XXXXXXXXXXXXXXXXX.
    "XXXXXXXXXX. XXXXXXXXXXXX. XXXXXXXXXXX."
XXXXXXXXXXXXXXXXX.
    "XXXXXXXXXX. XXXXXXXXXXXX. XXXXXXXXXXX."
XXXXXXXXXXX. XXXXXXXXXXX. XXXXXXXXXXXX
XXXXXXXXXX. "This is the best experience I have ever had,"
Jones said.

- The "To-Be-Continued" Series: Here the writer has material of an A & B nature, or subtopics 1, 2, & 3. The "to-be-continued" series summarizes the A & B, or the 1, 2, 3, then discusses the topics individually.
  Here would be an example of the "to-be-continued" series:

  > Smith's life is highlighted by his success in three areas: his home and stable family life; his career at Allied Microcomputer and his hobby as an acclaimed landscape painter.
  > At home, he _____
  > _____.
  > At Allied Microcomputer, his success has been _____
  > _____.
  > And his landscape paintings have won awards throughout the country and are in private collections _____.

- The Time Transition: This is a simple technique:

  > "In February, 1986, Vice-President Bush has decided to . . . ."
  > "By late 1986, Bush had accomplished. . . ."

  This offers a quick and clean transition into an anecdote or other subtopic within your article.

- The Dialogue: Let one personality (A) in your article make a statement: Let another personality (B) answer as a way to transition from (A) to a subtopic about (B):

  > "I think such-and-such is true," "A" said finally, resting his arms on the table and looking out the window. "I've just always believed that."

  >   *   *   *

  > "I just don't believe in such-and-such at all," "B" said later. "That's never been true as far as I am concerned."
  > B's life, from the early 1940s, indicates that _____.

- The Concluding Statement: Here a quotation or statement by the writer effectively draws a section to a close:

  > "The one thing I have always wanted to be in my life is the high school coach of the Hutto, Texas, Hippos," he said.

TRANSITIONAL SIGNALS

In *The Random House Handbook,* Crews (1980) also wrote:

> Signals of *transition* indicate that the *previous statement will be expanded, supported, or qualified in some say.* Those signals consist of all the words and phrases that show how a statement will build on a previous one. The types of transition, with a few examples of each type are:
>
> Consequence:
> Therefore, then, thus, hence, accordingly, as a result
> Likeness:
> Likewise, similarly
> Contrast:
> But, however, nevertheless, on the contrary, on the other hand, yet
> Amplification:
> And, again, in addition, further, furthermore, moreover, also, too
> Example:
> For instance, for example
> Concession:
> To be sure, granted, of course, it is true
> Insistence:
> Indeed, in fact, yes, no
> Sequence:
> First, Second, finally
> Restatement:
> That is, in other words, in simpler terms, to put it differently
> Recapitulation:
> In conclusion, all in all, to summarize, altogether
> Time or Place:
> Afterward, later, earlier, formerly, elsewhere, here, there, hitherto, subsequently, at the same time, simultaneously, above, below, farther on, this time, so far, until now. (pp. 112–113)

Of these phrases, Crews wrote, "Such signals needn't appear in every sentence, but they become useful wherever the relationship between two sentences would be immediately clear without them" (p. 113).

FOUR KEY STORY STRUCTURES

In general, there are four *types* of construction that writers use: the Inverted Pyramid, the Diamond or News-Magazine for, *The Wall Street Journal* form, and a modified Diamond for.

Each type has some advantages and some disadvantages.

The Inverted Pyramid form is most popular in newspapers. The Diamond form is most effective for personality profiles, or articles that have an "historical background" section. The Diamond form is recognizable in many magazines.

The Wall Street Journal formula is very effective for story topics that may be illustrated by focusing in the beginning *and at the end of the article* on an individual. (This formula is also effective for "debate"-type articles, in which the writer suggests a *premise* at the beginning, *proof* in the middle, and a *conclusion* at the end of a three-segment article.)

Modified forms are articles in which the Diamond formula has been altered. Shown later is a Diamond formula article with a specific *Diary* form in the middle of the article.

Each deserves individual analysis. We present an example and a discussion of each (and a diagram of the first three types).

The Front-Page Newspaper or "Inverted Pyramid" Structure

This structure or form is invariably discussed in journalism schools as an "Inverted Pyramid," and, if you wish to use a geometric symbol, the inverted pyramid, or "upside-down triangle" is a valid representation of this form.

This form is top heavy with key facts, figures, dates, and quotations at the top of the article.

Major facts, quotations, details, and descriptions follow after the lead. The writer uses all the major details toward the top of the article and works toward the bottom of the article using major-to-minor facts.

The facts become less and less important toward the bottom of the article.

This form or style serves two important functions: (a) it *informs* the reader at the top of the story of the key details and (b) the story could be cut apart toward the end without crippling the meaning of the story.

This has great advantages to newspaper editors who may be working on designing a front page as a "disaster story" is moved to the newspaper on the AP or UPI wires. If an editor has 5 minutes to go to press with the front page and if the story *deserves* to be placed on the front page, the editor may cut 3 inches from a 12-inch story if there are only 9 inches of space available on the front page.

Editors used to literally cut stories apart—now they can be cut apart on computer screens instantly. The rest of the story may be killed, or, may disappear electronically, to be "called back" if the editor wants to use the longer version of the story "jumping" the rest of the copy to an inside page.

There are two key disadvantages to this inverted pyramid story, both worth discussing:

- First, because the story is "top heavy" with key facts, details, and quotations in the top of the story, major details in the middle of the story and minor details at the bottom of the story, *this type of story will never become more interesting, more valuable or more involving than it is at the beginning.*

These stories get progressively *less and less valuable* and *less and less interesting* as they go on.

Some journalism school professors suggest these stories "dribble down the front page" and in fact they do.

• Second, there is no "space available" in these stories for any real background. All of these stories are assumed—if they are on today's front page—to have happened yesterday. Everything is *immediate.* If a reporter needs to explain what happened 20 years ago in a particular field, it is generally easier to write a separate story than it would be to try and fit that kind of detailed background into an Inverted Pyramid story. Journalists often used the term *Backgrounder* to identify separate stories that explain the history of a specific topic.

Finally, these Inverted Pyramid stories are all "one-piece" stories, whether they are 9 paragraphs long, 19, or 39. Newspaper editors may use spacebreaks with long stories, but they are still written top-to-bottom, important-to-trivial in one logical line.

In *Newswriting: From Lead to "30,"* William Metz (1979) wrote:

> For all its utility and general-purpose value, the inverted pyramid has its critics. It has been rapped for being overstandardized and lacking in variety. The pyramid is not a natural storytelling method, its detractors say, because the climax comes at the outset; moreover, they contend, the style is predictable and old-fashioned. And Roger Tatarian, former editor of United Press International, has predicted that narrative leads will increase in popularity over summary leads, especially in stories that the reader has already heard over the air.
>
> There is some truth to this. But it seems safe to replay that the traditional inverted-pyramid patter will continue to dominate in the unadorned presentation of facts. Young reporters would do well to master it before going on to more sophisticated literary devices. Even with the inverted pyramid, there is plenty of opportunity for a writer to demonstrate his command of the language, his imagination and his originality. The by-line stars of the wire services and the syndicates don't often begin their features with inverted pyramids, but you can bet that's how they wrote their first stories. (p. 72)

Name: Inverted Pyramid form.

Advantages: Ideal for "front-page" stories—disasters, fires, accidents; used for almost all basic newspaper articles as well, except for columns, editorials, and miscellaneous material.

Disdvantages: Gets less and less interesting, less and less valuable; no room for historical background. Weak ending.

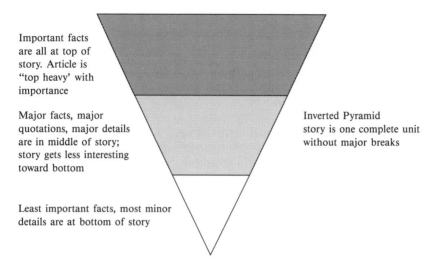

Important facts are all at top of story. Article is "top heavy' with importance

Major facts, major quotations, major details are in middle of story; story gets less interesting toward bottom

Inverted Pyramid story is one complete unit without major breaks

Least important facts, most minor details are at bottom of story

FIG. 2.1. Inverted pyramid structure

This Associated Press article is a perfect example of an Inverted Pyramid news story. It appeared in *The Dallas Morning News* Feb. 16, 1987.

10 die as 2 planes collide
over Salt Lake City area

Friday, January 16, 1987

Typical summary news lead

Salt Lake City (AP)—A commuter aircraft that was preparing to land and a private plane on a training flight collided over the Salt Lake Valley on Thursday, killing all 10 people aboard and showering debris over a residential area, authorities said.

Lead continues for two additional paragraphs

Falling wreckage from the twin-engine Skywest Metroliner and the private plane damaged three houses, but there were no fires and apparently no one on the ground was hurt, said Salt Lake County Fire Marshal Frank Brown.

Dozens of police, sheriff's deputies and firefighters rushed to the snowy crash site about 15 miles southwest of downtown Salt Lake City, and cordoned off six blocks of the neighborhood after the 12:56 p.m. collision.

First key quotation by an official

"They are picking up bodies here and there, whenever people call us to report them," Brown said.

There was initial confusion over the death toll as bodies were scattered through the neighborhood in the unincorporated community of Kearns. By nightfall, authorities had found nine of the 10 bodies, said Salt Lake County Sheriff Pete Hayward.

Background details

The accident was the first U.S. Commercial aviation disaster of the year. It came at a time of increasing concern over air safety

in the wake of an Aug. 31, 1986, collision over Cerritos, Calif.,
of a private plane and a Aeromexico DC-9 jetliner that killed
82 people.

Skywest Flight 18 was carrying six passengers and a crew of
two from Pocatello, Idaho, to Salt Lake International Airport,
said Ron Weber, a Skywest vice president. The turboprop aircraft can carry 18 passengers and two crew members.

The other plane, a blue-and-white Mooney M-20 with a student pilot and flight instructor aboard, had taken off 26 minutes
before the collision from nearby Airport No. 2, a small facility
that is used primarily by light aircraft and sometimes by planes
diverted from the Salt Lake City International Airport.

The Skywest plane was about to turn into its final approach
to the larger airport when the accident occurred, said Tom Doyle,
Salt Lake International Airport assistant air traffic controller.

"We were working him on our radar. We had not (yet) handed
him off to the tower for a visual approach. We had just turned
him on what we call a base leg, which is perpendicular to his
flight path inboard. . . . The next turn would have been direct
to the runway," Doyle said.

An Airport No. 2 official, who declined to be identified but
said he spoke for base operator Ron Nelson, said the four-seat
Mooney took off from the airport in West Jordan at 12:30 p.m.
on what was apparently a training flight.

Witnesses on the ground said they heard a "boom" and then
saw parts of the planes showering to the ground.

"I looked up and there was just parts flying all over," said
Martin Bee of Kearns. "You couldn't tell one thing or another.
You couldn't tell what was what. I was just ducking and trying
to stay out of the way of things."

"It went 'Boom!' and the whole house was shaken really badly," said Rebecca Whitelock. "It was like a major earthquake,
and I opened the bedroom door and there were wheels sticking
out of the bedroom."

In Washington, the Federal Aviation Administration said the
Skywest plane disappeared from radar four minutes before the
crash while flying at 7,000 feet about eight miles southwest of
the main Salt Lake City airport.

Visibility at the time was 30 miles with a cloud ceiling of 7,000
feet, according to FAA spokesman Fred Farrar in Washington.
Winds up to 60 mph were whipping through the area shortly
afterward.

The largest piece of the wreckage, the Metroliner's fuselage,
fell in the middle of a snow-covered street. Fire Battalion Chief
John Corak said there were four bodies inside.

A temporary morgue and command post were set up at St.
Francis Xavier Catholic Church, where parts of bodies fell in
the parking lot and on the steps of a nearby church-run school,
said sheriff's Lt. Bill A. Van Wagenen.

The identities of the victims were not immediately available.
Sister Marilyn Mark, a teacher at St. Francis Xavier, said she
was sitting in her office and "I thought someone was shoveling
snow on the roof. Seconds later, I heard a kind of crash. I ran
downstairs to see what was going on. That's when I found a part
of a body. It seemed to be a leg."

The 80 students were evacuated uninjured from the area.

Investigators from the FAA and National Transportation
Safety Board went to the scene.

The tail sections of the planes were found among the debris
that was scattered in yards and streets over a wide area, said
Brown, the county fire marshall. One large piece of wreckage
was found embedded in a house, he added. (p. 1)

*Most
minor
details
& quotes
continue
to end
of story*

The Diamond or News-Magazine Form

This form is markedly and obviously different from the Inverted Pyramid.
In this form, the opening of the story is just that: a window, revealing *part*
of the story to the reader. It should be entertaining, educational, and infor-
mative, but it is still just an opening. The opening or lead of a news story
in the Inverted Pyramid may be three paragraphs long or perhaps as many
as six paragraphs long; there is no specific limit to the length of a beginning
in this Diamond form.

And instead of getting progressively less and less valuable as the story goes
on, as in the Inverted Pyramid, this form *gets more and more detailed, more
and more valuable, more and more complex.*

Instead of being one complete story, top-to-bottom as the Inverted
Pyramid stories usually are, the Diamond form has three parts: the opening, then a break, the middle of the story, and a break and then the end
segment.

If the writer uses this form correctly, the end cannot be cut apart and electronically "thrown away" as editors often do with Inverted Pyramid stories:
The end of a Diamond form story must be used. The end has *almost as much
impact* as the opening. To cut off the end of these stories means crippling
the effectiveness of this form.

If the Inverted Pyramid story is written in the present (everything on the
front page of today's newspapers happened yesterday), the Diamond form
story does allow the writer to "go back" to explain what happened last year,
or 10 years ago, or even—depending on the story—what happened 100 years
ago, if that is relevant and necessary to the story.

The "time" in an Inverted Pyramid story is thus:

NOW
NOW
NOW

throughout the whole story. The "now" being, for all practical purposes, yesterday, for today's front pages.

The "time" in a diamond form story is thus:

NOW
(in the beginning of story)
to
DISTANT PAST
(to)
NOW
(and end of story)

If such a story has to be cut or trimmed to fit space available in a publication, an editor will have to judiciously cut *in the middle* of the story, to avoid losing the flow of the present-to-past-to-present structure of this form.

This is sometimes called the "News-magazine form" because *Time* and *Newsweek* often use this form for their cover stories. The beginning tells why individual "X" is in the news and why he or she deserves to be on the cover; the story jumps to the historical background—then works up to date again through the individual's life story. Present-to-past-to-present.

The middle of this form offers the writer the opportunity to use anecdotes, sections devoted to personalities "A," "B," "C," "D," and others—offering a rich mix of facts, quotation, history, description and details.

In contrast to the Inverted Pyramid form, this form should become more and more interesting to the reader, not less and less interesting.

If the writer starts with personality "A," works through the article *and ends with personality "A,"* the reader should be *instinctively satisfied because the writer has "come full circle"* in terms of time and in terms of subject, thus:

Present	—and—	Personality "A"
(to)		(to)
Distant Past	—or—	Personality "B"
(to)		(to)
Recent Past	—or—	Personality "C"
(to)		(to)
Present	—and—	Personality "A"

The writer begins and ends in the present, begins and ends with Personality "A"—in short begins and ends where the article started.

Name: Diamond or News-magazine form.

Advantages: Offers opportunity for present in the beginning in and end, past in the upper middle of the article. Perfect for personality profiles. Should have strong, empathetic ending.

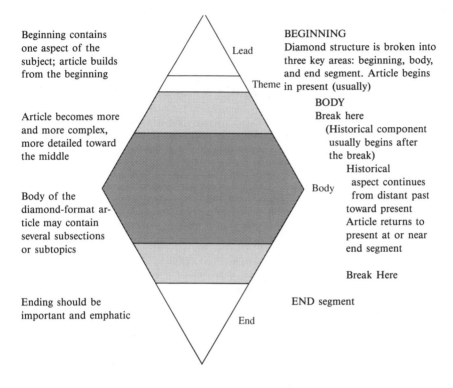

FIG. 2.2. Diamond or news-magazine structure

Disadvantages: More complicated to construct. Writers should use outline as a roadmap for ease of planning.

The following article by Jack Evans (1986) was written in a University of Texas Advanced Feature Writing class. It was published in *The Daily Texan* and subsequently entered in the annual William Randolph Hearst contest for college journalists.

In early 1987, it won First Place in Feature Writing, in the Hearst Contest for 1986.

Evans' profile is a touching one; he begins with Teddy's funeral, moves back in time a year to the latter stages of Teddy's illness and moves forward again. Evans ends Teddy's story where it began.

Teddy

A chronicle of the final days
of a 29-year-old AIDS victim

by Jack Evans

Evans' lead:
Teddy's
funeral
May 24,
1986

The orange glow intensifies and blankets Corpus Christi Bay as the sun ever so slowly edges its way toward the crevice separating ocean from sky. Sunset, May 24, 1986. Twenty or so passengers gather at the rear of the charter boat, passing back small paper cups. They shield them with their hands, careful not to let the wind disturb the powdery contents. Near the railing Dub Daugherty fills another with ash from a large brass urn.

Terry Lee "Teddy" Langley had once weighed 180 pounds and stood 5 feet 10 inches tall. Now, his ashen remains barely fill a container the size of a 2-pound coffee can.

*   *   *

The lead
continues,
after a
spacebreak

One by one, the passengers approach the railing and pour the contents into the bay. Slivers of bone sink quickly from sight while the ashes sift slowly into the waves.

Everything went according to plan—Teddy's plan. He knew this final scenario all too well, because for 372 days he played it out in his head again and again as his body wasted away.

Good short
sentence,
followed
by key
paragraph
of facts

Teddy was a victim of AIDS.

Since 1981, when acquired immune deficiency syndrome was first diagnosed in the United States, 24,859 cases of the disease have been reported. So far, 13,689 people diagnosed with AIDS have died, 50 percent within the first year of contracting the disease.

Another
key
sentence

Teddy beat the odds, but only by seven days.

*   *   *

A
flashback,
a year
earlier

It's almost springtime. March, 1985. A Talking Heads song blares from the banged-up jukebox in the back room of Buddy's Ice Box, an ice house north of downtown San Antonio. Part outdoor beer garden and part neighborhood grocery, Buddy's attracts a diverse clientele: delivery drivers and upwardly mobile accountants, street-wise philosophers and new wave pseudo-intellectuals, young Mexican toughs and earringed homosexuals.

Tonight the cool outdoor air keeps the small crowd of patrons inside, talking and laughing over the muffled beat of the music.

Near the front window, Teddy stands talking with some friends at a table. Outwardly, he seems healthy. See his broad smile and the rosy glow of his handsome young cheeks? See how his muscular arms gesture animatedly as he talks?

But look at his eyes. See the glazed stare beneath the heavy hung eyelids? This is a symptom of what Teddy calls his "self-destructive binge." Lately, he's been drinking and doing a lot of drugs, hanging out at bars all night and sleeping around. But he's having a good time, right? Watch him joke and laugh with his friends. See? Everything is all right.

Hard to imagine that in less than a month Teddy will be in a hospital with tubes up his nose and IVs rooted in his forearms.

In just a few short weeks, Teddy will visit a friend's house and will become dizzy and short of breath, soon finding it so hard to breathe that his friend will take him to the hospital.

And then Teddy will learn from his doctors he has been diagnosed with AIDS, and from that moment on, his entire life will change.

*   *   *

A jump forward in time— 6 months

The raging Texas summer shows no signs of giving up to the approaching fall. September, 1985. Teddy isn't giving in either. In and out of the hospital during the past few months, Teddy is showing signs of improvement. His weight has increased to 153 pounds, up 15 pounds or so. His frame is a gaunt and sunken shadow of its former self; however, Teddy is trying to remain cheerful.

It is Sunday. Services about to begin at River City Living Church, a non-denominational church with a mostly gay congregation. Daugherty, the president of the church's administrative council, has taken Teddy into his home and the church helps purchase Teddy's prescriptions. Teddy is broke and draws only Social Security insurance. Just six days before he would have qualified for medical coverage at his last job, Teddy came down with AIDS.

"I've had to modify my lifestyle because of AIDS," a member of the congregation says during a brief testimonial. Many here share his concern, largely because 70 percent of all AIDS victims are gay and bisexual men. Later as the congregation stands in a prayer circle, the pastor asks for continued health for Teddy and AIDS patients everywhere.

After the closing hymn is sung, *Pass It On,* a member of the congregation quips quietly, "The word is not to pass it on these days."

*   *   *

Christmas is just two weeks away. December, 1985. Teddy and some of Dub's housemates are trimming the Christmas tree. Teddy and John are stringing up the lights while Ray, the church's administrative secretary, untangles ornaments.

John asks to be referred to only by his first name, while Ray asks that his real name not be used. Both fear their gay lifestyles and participation in the church could threaten their job security.

"You know what I'd like to do," Teddy says from atop a stool as he wraps a string of lights around the uppermost branches of the tree. "I'd like to just get lost in a city somewhere. New York maybe, for Christmas. I'd just go somewhere where I don't know anybody and nobody knew me and wander around taking pictures. That's what I'd like to do."

Since September, Teddy has been hospitalized only once, after suffering a seizure at the house. He's also contracted a rare form of bone tuberculosis.

"I'm tired of being treated like an AIDS patient," Teddy says in a more serious tone. "As soon as I found out I had AIDS people immediately started treating me differently. I think mostly because they were scared, afraid."

"He's a leper," John interjects. "That's what society has turned him into."

Teddy pauses. "My sisters and aunts—I went to a family dinner with them and while everybody else was served with china I got a plastic plate. People greet me with straight arm handshakes. You're not going to get AIDS from casual contact.

"I called my father to talk to him about it and he wouldn't even, wasn't brave enough to call me back."

Teddy explains he was in a much higher risk group than most AIDS victims because he was both a homosexual and an intravenous drug user.

"I think I got it from the needle. I shared a lot of needles. Lots of drugs with lots of friends," Teddy says.

"I remember once I decided to clean myself up and dumped all my drugs and syringes and needles in the garbage. Later, I found some crank in a drawer and wanted it so bad I went to the garbage dumpster and dug through the trash until I found the needle, then just rinsed it with water and used it.

"Drugs. They will tear you down."

Another key paragraph of facts

Seventeen percent of all AIDS patients are intravenous drug abusers, while 2 percent are hemophiliacs and people who have had blood transfusions. About one percent of all cases are heterosexuals.

Teddy steps down from the stool and walks over to the couch. He sits down and sips from a glass of Sprite.

"A couple of people I had slept with called me up as soon as I got it. Here I am with tubes running out of me, flat on my back in a hospital bed, and people are calling me up saying 'You gave me AIDS.'

"But a lot of people I knew were sympathetic. I mean, AIDS doesn't make me any less human. I don't deserve to be treated as if I deserved to get AIDS. There are people out there who think, 'You dirty faggot, serves you right to get AIDS.'"

"God's will," Ray says sarcastically.

"You know," Ray continues, "I remember when my aunt and my sister contracted tuberculosis when I was a child. My mother was the only one to go visit them. It didn't make any difference what they were sick from, they were family, they were people that needed to be cared for."

Teddy shakes his head. "When I had my first seizure here at the house, they had to call an ambulance," Teddy recalls. "One of the EMS technicians refused to touch me as soon as he learned I had AIDS. And in the hospital the orderlies gave me problems. They acted as if pushing me down the hall in a wheelchair was going to kill them. Seriously.

"These are health care people."

Teddy walks back over to the tree.

"I remember once, though, when I was in the hospital," Teddy continues, "this nurse and I got to talking one night for a long time. She showed me pictures of her family. She really cared about how I was doing. Later she wrote me a letter. It was one of the loveliest letters I've ever gotten and it was from someone who was basically a perfect stranger. No one in my family has written anything like that."

*   *   *

Another section: the chronology moves forward again

Springtime comes unexpectedly early. March 1986. The oxygen regulator hisses in the background in the seventh floor room of the Methodist Hospital. An ice blanket cools Teddy's feverish body, which heaves violently with each hoarse breath. He sleeps nonetheless. A silent onlooker sits motionless in a chair at the side of the bed.

Teddy had been in the hospital now for a week and a half. This morning he was moved to the intermediate care unit where he continued to receive treatment for pneumocystis carinii pneumonia. Usually only seen in cancer or transplant patients taking certain types of drugs, the disease is caused by a parasite. It is the leading cause of death in AIDS patients. This is not Teddy's first bout with this form of pneumonia.

A sign on the door bears an infectious disease warning, which is meant to protect Teddy more than visitors. A simple cold brought in from outside could be fatal because of his weakened immune system. The greatest threat to outsiders is for those who have already contracted the AIDS virus and could be infected with the pneumonia.

Around the edges of the room are bins and containers for contaminated linens and body fluids. When drawing blood or performing activities which could bring nurses and doctors in contact with bodily fluids, gloves are worn.

Teddy's eyelids flutter.

"Teddy, are you awake?" Dub asks.

Slowly his eyes open wide and he stares hard at his visitor. As the feverish confusion clears from his head he recognizes Dub. They share a few words as Teddy wheezes painfully until a nurse enters the room and tells him to conserve his energy.

"We've tried to have someone here at the hospital just to be around and keep him company," Dub whispers. "It makes him feel like he's not alone and I really think it helps him.

"He is strong. Not very much so emotionally, but physically. If we can be here to offer solace it makes him stronger."

Dub has known Teddy for six years.

He was a very high energy type of person. He was a lot of fun to be around. But he doesn't have that same level of energy any more.

"I've had people ask me if I thought I was risking my health to have him around. I refuse to treat him like a leper. That kind of fear affects you psychologically. And Teddy doesn't need that. He needs people that care.

"What do I get out of it? Basically, it gives me a chance to practice everything I was taught about how you treat other people. Talk is cheap. If you talk about being a Christian you should start doing."

Teddy's hand shakes as he reaches for the glass on the side of the table. As he leans forward to drink from his plastic straw, his neck trembles. So much strength for so little a sip.

"All I want is to wake up someday without any aches or pains," Teddy says as the nurse approaches his bed. In a few moments, Valium streams from the IV into his arm, returning him to a fog of drug-induced sedation.

*   *   *

Evans moves past the opening, for a summary section

Four and a half months have passed since Teddy died. September, 1986. Dub and John are working late at the church, putting labels on letters to be mailed the following morning. The congregation is trying to raise money for a new building close by.

Twenty-two days after Teddy died, Hugh, another AIDS patient living at Dub's house passed away. One of the longest surviving AIDS patients, Hugh had lived with the disease for 3½ years.

"It's ironic," Dub says, "around Christmas, Teddy was starting to gain weight and look better and Hugh said, 'Teddy, you really are in good shape. Better take care of yourself. You're in good shape.' Four months later Teddy died."

Teddy's final stay in the hospital lasted 61 days. He had contracted pneumocystis pneumonia four times. Most AIDS patients die after contracting the pneumonia once.

"The Tuesday before he died he seemed to be doing better," Dub explains. "He hadn't been getting enough oxygen up until then. But he seemed to be doing OK that night.

"But after I left, he got up in the middle of the night and the nurses faintly heard him calling, 'Nurse, nurse.' When they went to his room, he had gotten out of be on his own and sat down in a chair in the room. He told them he wanted to go home and die.

"He said he was going to be with Momma Helen, his grandmother, the night he died. He knew he was dying," Dub said.

*   *   *

Evans returns to the opening scene— Teddy's funeral—

As the sun slips out of sight, the boat's passengers open a case of champagne, and the group of friends and family toast Teddy's memory. Afterward, they cast 2½ dozen red and white carnations into the water.

In the distance, the city lights of Corpus Christi shine brightly on the horizon. For the last time, Teddy was returned home to

for a   the bay, where as a small boy he sat alongside his grandparents
poignant   and fished away the afternoons of his childhood. (Images sec-
end   tion, p. 1)

Earlier we wrote "the Diamond form story does allow the writer to "go back" to explain what happened last year, or 10 years ago, or even—depending on the story—what happened 100 years ago, if that is relevant and necessary to the story."

The following story "goes back" 100 years.

"Lookin' for a good bowl of red?" (Fensch, 1983) is a regional story, published in a national magazine. It explains the special love that Texans have for chili and, in the historical segment, shows how chili came to be.

Like "Teddy," this article has extensive quotations and details, but the historical jump is different, and this story contains definitions *chiliheads* use; quotations from books about chili and even recipes.

Because the story is long and detailed a newspaper *dateline* is used when the article returns to the present—in this case the world's largest chili cookoff, held annually in San Marcos, Texas.

"Teddy" and "Lookin' for a good bowl of red?" are presented together to show how appropriate the Diamond format is for a wide variety of subjects—from personality portraits to *subject* articles like chili cooking. *Internally,* both articles show the same present-to-past-to-present formula. That formula allows "room" inside the article for various subtopics.

(Incidentally, the outline for the chili article, typed single-spaced, was almost a full-page long.)

Looking' for a good bowl of red?

The pomp and circumstances of
chili cooking from some of the
world's best chili cooks . . .

by Thomas Fensch, from *Cavalier* magazine

A state-   In a state which often considers itself a separate nation in
ment begin-   terms of size, wealth, population and influence, chili is "the na-
ning is   tional dish of Texas."
used for   It is a dish that is as old as the Alamo, as native as Longhorn
this article   cattle, as durable as the mountains, as comfortable as an old
                pair of boots and often hotter than a border town Saturday night.

A break   Buzzard's Breath chili, Nevada Annie's Cowboy chili, Sun
shows the   Dance chili, Reno Red chili, Pecos River Bowl of Red chili, Ar-
variety of   madillo chili, Gringo chili, Navajo Green chili, Dirty Leg chili,
chili recipes   Cow Chip chili, Top Secret chili . . .

This is a   What is chili? There are as many answers as there are chili
disguised   cooks:
list of   John "Bad McFad" Raven, Temple, Texas: "Chili is a meat
definitions   dish spiced with chili peppers." Fair enough.

"It's . . . it's . . . mostly a big mess, you know, It just gets real messy, with meat, sauces, salts and spices. I don't know how you'd characterize it, it's just kind messy."—James P. O'Hara, Houston.

Davis Lewis, Wimberly, Texas: "It's a concoction made only in Texas . . . it's made with sometimes fresh ingredients. We have a secret recipe that has been handed down from generation to generation. I've added my two cents to it. . . ."

Then there is this chili:

"We take the testicles from a male bovine and skin 'em and slice 'em up and fry 'em. Mountain Oysters. We take these aforementioned and add 'em to chili. They kinda mellow out the peppers to just the right hotness. Is that a word?"

Does this improve the performance of males who eat this chili?

"You bet . . . they seem to think so and as long as they think so, we'll keep feedin' it to 'em . . ."—Mountain Oyster Bar team members, Luling and San Marcos, Texas.

"This is your basic beef stock. You can't have it too greasy or too tomatoey, or too runny. We put venison in it and filet mignon, we put in 34 doves, we put rabbit in it and quail. And squirrel. We call it your basic beef stew chili."—Yo' Mamma's chili team.

Summary
paragraph

Good Texas chili is meats, spices, salts, sauces and a large, large, helping of Texas bullshit.

Red Jurecka, San Marcos, Texas: "Chili is cumino (cumin—a Mexican spice), meat, onions, garlic, jalapenos (peppers), tomato sauce, pepper and salt, oregano and a secret ingredient. Those are the basics. . . ."

Here is a
question a
reader might
have—and
the answer

What's the secret ingredient?

"I'm not going to tell you."

Larry Otto, Llano, Texas: Chili is "meat. You can cut it up by hand. Into chunks. Add spices. Some people like to add other garbage, but basically it's nothing but meat and spices . . . it's a way of life for me. I've been cookin' chili ever since I was a kid. I was raised on chili. That's no joke. . . ."

Tex Schofield, New Braunfels, Texas, All-Time, Lifetime, Exalted, Majestic Supreme Grand Chili Pepper (chili official): "Chili is an aphrodisiac. (Schofield doesn't pronounce it in the usual *chilley* but chil-*lie*.) It is a group of herbs, spices, meats—some of which may be purchased at the grocery store or scraped off the highway—and a secret ingredient. Chili cooks who consistently place in the high categories of chili cooking will not reveal what their secret ingredients are. Of course, I realize that Tabasco brand of hot sauce is probably one of the best secret ingredients known to mankind. So it's basically an aphrodisiac, which is not a luxury, it's a necessary; it's a staple for anyone who wants to have a long and healthy life."

And this, from Lady Bird Johnson, who was quoted in Frank X. Tolbert's book *A Bowl of Red,* while her husband Lyndon Johnson was president: "My feeling about chili is this—along in November when the first Norther (Texas winter storm) strikes, and the skies are grey, along about five o'clock in the afternoon, I get to thinking how good chili would taste for supper. It always lives up to expectations. In fact, you don't even mind the cold November winds."

Super Bowl Chili

Note: If you quote an entire recipe or poem, make sure you have written permission from the copyright holder

4 pounds flank or round steak, cubed
3 pounds chili-grind chuck
3 large onions, chopped
3 tablespoons garlic, finely chopped
2 tablespoons vinegar
3 tablespoons oregano
5 tablespoons cumin
2 tablespoons instant coffee
3 tablespoons paprika
2 tablespoons sugar
2 tablespoons coriander
2 tablespoons table mustard
7-9 tablespoons chili powder
3 soup cans beef broth
1 No. 2 can tomatoes, mashed
1 soup can tomato sauce
2 bell peppers, put through food processor
2 bay leaves
3 jalapeno peppers (canned), but through food processor
Salt and pepper to taste
Red pepper to taste
2 pinches Williams seasoning (anything else that occurs to you)
Brown onion, garlic and meat. Dump everything else in a large pot and simmer about 5 hours. Will serve 14-16 men. Freezes well.—Dick Williams, Austin.

Historical background begins here—article jumps back about 100 years

Contrary to popular belief, chili (or chil-*lie*) is not a Mexican dish. The Mexicans have a red pepper dish and a green pepper dish or stew, but nothing exactly like chili. In fact, there is considerable evidence that chili was born in San Antonio, Texas, or thereabouts, in the late 1800s. During that time, the poorer residents of San Antonio bought the cheapest meat available and added spices and herbs to make it go as far as possible. Since the meat was cheap, the flavor was lacking and the spices helped make the meat taste better. Because many traditional vegetables don't grow well in Texas because of the heat—it is often 100 during the summers in San Antonio and central Texas— citizens used the herbs and spices which did like the Texas sun. Chili peppers, jalapenos and Mexican peppers. Unknowingly, they were also aiding their diet—peppers are rich in vitamins A and C.

Another fable has it that jailers used a thin gruel of meat and water and flour to feed inmates in Texas, and spiced that with salt, pepper, onions and whatever spicey chilies which were available. Thus today, there are many versions of jailhouse chili around and many Sheriffs today serve jailhouse chili to inmates in the local slammer. . . .

Another fable, which probably contains more truth tells that the trailriders—the old, original cowboys—who rode from San Antonio north past Austin toward Dallas or Fort Worth on the famous Chisholm Trail, used to take a couple of cows along with the herd, toward the cattle centers of Kansas and the midwest. One cow, properly butchered, would last a long time on the trail and feed considerable numbers of cowboys. But there was little refrigeration—no refrigeration really—and the butchered cow would soon get gamey—the spices, and chilies would help keep the meat eatable.

Range cooks who didn't read and probably didn't write either—having little use for either—had to experiment with their recipes and memorize their best attempts at chili. Best recipes were kept secret because a good range cook was hard to find and cooks didn't trade recipes when they had good one. There are about 300 varieties of chili peppers, from the very mild to the very hottest and one cook could rightly assert that he had a secret recipe which included one kind of pepper; another chili cook would claim another kind of pepper was better. Green chili peppers are not ripe and have a tarter flavor; red peppers are ripe and have a mellower flavor. Powdered chili peppers keep well, so range cooks could spice up any kind of semieatable meat with chili peppers, onions, salt and regular black pepper to make a satisfying meal in the cold winters.

History moves to 1940s

From the late 1800s until about 1943, chili was everywhere in San Antonio. Near Alamo, "chili queens," ladies with small carts, decorated with lights, served chili in community bowls. The chili queens lent a festive air: occasionally they literally fought for the right streetcorner. In the 1940s, city fathers closed down the chili queens; because of the passed-along bowls, the chili wagons were banned for "unsanitary conditions," which were probably more sanitary than the original trailcooks and their semi-fresh meat.

A jump back in time for a subtopic: canned chili

While the chili queens were cooking and serving in downtown San Antonio, others were discovering how to make small fortunes with chili—by canning it. Gebhardt's chili was begun in 1908 and grew steadily since then. Wolf Brand chili was begun in 1885, but only began real sales about 1921 when Lyman Davis began to can it in quantity and sell it to Texas storeowners from a Model T; the car and others like it driven by other Wolf Brand salesmen were decorated to resemble chili cans; the wolf on the can was "Kaiser Bill," a pet wolf once owned by Davis. Prepared chili powder was also developed about the same time, but in Fort Worth by DeWitt Clinton Pendery. Pendery and William Gebhardt are now known as the "powder men" of chili history.

Note: if you are reprinting a recipe, proofread carefully so nothing is changed or left out

Lyndon and Lady Bird Johnson's
Pedernales (pear-din-alice) River Chili

3 tablespoons lard or bacon drippings
4 pounds lean beef, coarse chili grind
1 large onion, coarsely chopped
2 medium cloves garlic, finely chopped
3 teaspoons salt
1 teaspoon dried oregano (preferably Mexican)
1 teaspoon ground cumin
2 cups boiling water
1 32-ounce can whole tomatoes
4 tablespoons ground hot red chile
2 tablespoons ground mild red chile

1. Melt the lard or bacon drippings in a large saute pan over medium-high heat. Add the meat to the pan. Break up any lumps with a fork and cook, stirring occasionally until the meat is evenly browned.

2. Add the onions and garlic and cook until the onions are translucent.

3. Stir in the salt, oregano, cumin, water and tomatoes.

4. Gradually stir in the ground chile, testing until you achieve the degree of hotness and flavor that suits your palate. Bring to a boil, then lower heat and simmer, uncovered, for 1 hour. Stir occasionally.

Serves: 8

History moves into the 1960s

All this was B.T. Before Terlingua. The modern age of chili cooking—some say chili madness—began about 1966. That year *Dallas Morning News* columnist Frank X. Tolbert published the first edition of his book, *A Bowl of Red*. In August, 1977, humorist H. Allen Smith, living in Mt. Kisco, New York, author of *Low Man on a Totem Pole* and other books, published an article in *Holiday* magazine titled "Nobody Knows More About Chili Than I Do." Tolbert and his Texan friends had previously established the Chili Appreciation Society International (CASI) and Smith proceeded with great aplomb to take apart Tolbert, CASI, Texas chili and Texans. Smith wrote that CASI members were "childish, semi-rumpled Rotarian cracker-breakers, withered and pock-marked from eating that mud-puddin' Texans choose to call chili. . . ."

Another key summary paragraph

No one—by God—insults Texas, Texans, their men or women, their money, land, cattle or their chili. Especially their chili.

Tolbert, CASI members and other Texans challenged Smith to a chili duel. A cookoff. They made the date and place—Texas. Terlingua, Texas, the farthest place from anywhere in the state.

A fine quote here

One Texan has called Terlingua "almost next to nowhere," and with no Texas hyperbole, he is exactly right. Terlingua, a corruption of the original name, Tres Lingos, is a ghost town. Find El Paso on the Texas map, find the Big Bend country and near the Big Bend, you'll find Terlingua. One early cowboy characterized it as "You go south from Fort Davis until you come to (a) place where the rainbows wait for the rain and the mountains float in the air, except at night when they go away to play with other mountains. And the river is kept in big, stone boxes and water rolls uphill. . . ."

Terlingua is so far into the mountains that the lights on the desert make it appear that water does run uphill.

A first question a visitor to Terlingua might have is "How far is it to *somewhere*?" Alpine, Texas, is 82 miles and El Paso is much, much farther.

A favorite anecdote of mine

If not the easiest place to get to, Terlingua is perhaps the most appropriate for the chili cookoffs. Terlingua is reputed to have the deepest privies in the world. They are built at the top of abandoned mine shafts. Once comfortably seated in a Terlingua privy, a visitor is seat to be able to cup his hand "and hear Chinese community singing."

Before the first Terlingua cookoff, H. Allen Smith was offered a proclamation making him an honorary citizen of Texas. His reply: "I have no desire to behave in any honorable way during my stay in Texas."

Smith was matched against Austin cook Wick Fowler. One judge was clearly a Texan; one a New Yorker in favor of Smith's chili and a third judge, who is said to have gagged on one of the samples of chili and choked before he could reveal the loser—or the winner.

The first chili cookoff was a draw.

Thereafter, Texans who won smaller cookoffs were eligible to travel to Terlingua, as were other "foreigners," from California, New York and elsewhere. (H. Allen Smith attended other chili cookoffs and even eventually moved to Alpine, Texas.) Wick Fowler won in 1970, the first "honest" cookoff in terms of judging. And the mystique of chili cooking has been as much showmanship as gourmet cooking; gradually the showmanship got bigger. Now most cookoffs which are sponsored by CASI allow eight-man teams.

Terlingua is the World Series and the Super Bowl of chili all rolled into one: only in Texas would such an event be held year after year in the one place which is nearly inaccessible from anywhere in the civilized world. Fifty-one weeks of the year Terlingua is a ghost town; once a year chili cooks travel hundreds of miles to fry in the sun, freeze during the night, drink too much, then drive hundreds of hundreds of miles home. Only in Texas.

By the early 1970s, CASI had developed a 15-page list of chili rules, which are largely unknown by the average chili cook. Unwritten rules are known and rigidly observed. They are:

• Serious chili cooks *always* have a secret ingredient;

• Serious chili cooks *never* reveal their secret ingredient, even if it is only Tabasco sauce or some other common item;

• Most cookoffs are for men only. Women may not do so much as stir the chili pot as the chili is cooking. (This so enraged women cooks that they have formed their own society, the Hell-Hath-No-Fury-Like-A-Woman-Scorned chili society and they have their own cookoff in early October, in Luckenbach, Texas, population 3—*another ghost town*—near Fredericksburg, Texas.)

• Serious chili cooks *never* put beans in chili. The common rule is: one bean in a bowl of chili makes a bowl of beans. Chili with beans will be automatically disqualified from most CASI-sanctioned cookoffs.

• Hot chili *never* wins. If chili is hot enough to turn your face to cellophane or clear out your sinuses, it'll never win a CASI-sanctioned cookoff.

In general, chili is now judged on five observed categories:

• Color—it should be a deep red;

• Aroma;

• Consistency;

• The first taste—should be meaty and rich;

• The aftertaste—should make your throat glow.

No chili will win if it has beans; if it has gristle or mountain oysters, or armadillo or snake or anything else cooks "claim" to use; or is hot enough to make your eyes water or your nose run.

Since the late 1960s, CASI members have slowly developed their own slang: *chilihead,* chili cook or enthusiast; *red* or *a bowl of red,* chili; *pod,* local chapter of CASI.

Because of the length of this article, a newspaper

San Marcos, Texas, September 18, 1982—On a bare 17 acres surrounding the Hayes County Civic Coliseum, over 380 chili teams gather for the State of Texas' men's championship, the world's largest chili cookoff which carries an automatic seed to the world match in terlingua. No one ever gets a handle on how

"dateline"
is used to
bring the
reader back
to the
present

many teams enter the San Marcos Chiliympiad, as it is called. Early estimates place the number at 460; after-the-cookoff officials state 380. In the hot sun, with temperatures between 95 and 100, and not a tree in sight, with crowds estimated from 20,000 to 50,000, the Chiliympiad is for serious chili cooks; spectators should demand combat pay for braving the heat and the dust and the sun for the whole weekend.

Why bother? There are as many reasons for attending the Chiliympiad as there are cooks—or secret recipes. Red Jurecka, from San Marcos: "Cooking is fun—with the team members. You get a chance to meet the same people you see 'circuit chasing' (attending a regular schedule of cookoffs). You might meet the same people for two or three years until you know what they do (for a living). It can be an expensive hobby—with entry fees, and the costs of meats, spices and travel to each cookoff. Most chili cooks are of 'slight means'. . . ."

Jurecka is right. He is a college textbook salesman for the D.C. Heath Co.; Tex Schofield is a manufacturer's rep for a children's playground firm. John Raven is the maintenance officer for the Temple, Tx., police force. You don't have to be wealthy to cook chili—but it might help.

Many chili cooks who are veterans of 10 years or so of "circuit chasing," now deeply resent the "oilfield trash," equipment people, drilling rig companies, and "mud workers" who now invade the cookoffs and have plenty of money to spend on elaborate displays and who are now winning more and more showmanship awards. Their chili is something else again—few win big with their chili recipes.

John "Bad McFad" Raven is one of the true chiliheads who has been part of the chili-chasing circuit for the past ten years. Bad FcFad is a big boy 335-375, down from 400 to 450, and he used the name "Bad McFad" as a stage name. In a semi-literate drawl, McFad says, "I live for danger. . . ." At his upper weight, McFad could hardly waddle across the street. He has been in the top 10 at the Chiliympiad twice in the last 9 years.

Why do it? "I wandered down here ten years ago, lookin' for a hobby. I had so much fun with it, I have been here ever since. . . ." Bad McFad always has the best, choice location in the whole area: right in front of the judge's stage, where he can at once watch the judges—listen to Tex Schofield and watch all the t-shirts and the pretty girls. "There's no politics here at all— but I did go to school with the chairman. . . ."

Do you like to watch the girls and the short shorts and the bathing suits walk by? "I never notice—I'm too busy cooking— but I do take cold showers every 20 minutes. . . ."

His advice on chili cooking? "Buy the best ingredients, start with the smaller cookoffs, experiment with a recipe until you're satisfied with it and don't expect to win the big events right away. . . ."

David Schwartz, student financial aid officer at the University of Texas at Austin, cooking "No Frills chili" and wearing an apron which says, "A man's got to believe in something—I believe I'll have another drink" (W.C. Fields): "I've never cooked a bad bowl of chili. My original recipe was from a friend's mother. You have to experiment and change this, change that. I buy a special 'chili grind' meat. My chili is sometimes hotter than the judges would like, but it's what the people like. My chili is never as red as the judges like either, but then again these cookoffs are not always fair. It's said that some time ago, one cook put a sprig of parsley on top of his entry and the judges know which chili that was—another cook would carefully nick the edges of his entry cup. And the judges knew who *he* was. . . ."

Chili judging has not always had the decorum of the Supreme Court or the logic either. One famous woman chili judge, Kathy Morgan, was once in a severe auto accident. It is reported that she lost her sense of smell and *taste*. She went on being a chili judge anyway. Several years later, she had apparently *some* sense of taste restored, but no one knows for sure and she won't say one way or the other. (If you have the world's championship in two ghost towns, Terlingua and Luckenbach, you might as well have a judge without a sense of taste, too.)

Schwartz echoes Jurecka and Bad McFad regarding the expenses of chili cooking: "It costs $40 for the meats for one cookoff—for 12 pounds of meat. Spices cost $6-7; pepper, onions, garlic—another $2, then the entry fee for each cookoff ($25 at the Chiliympiad) and the cost of travel—it can get expensive if you let it."

And since there is a cookoff nearly every weekend, expenses can be very high.

*   *   *

How big has chili become? Shorty Fry, former rodeo clown and now business manager of Caliente Chili, in Austin (Drawer 5340, Austin, Tx., 78763), maker of Wick Fowler's Two-Alarm packaged chili said that Fowler began packaging his own secret recipe chili in the late 1960s and gave it to friends in and around Austin.

"One of Fowler's friends who ran a supermarket chain told Fowler that he'd like to sell it. That was the beginning. We have grown by 25-30 percent every year since the late 1960s. This year we'll ship 100,000 cases throughout the United States. We're getting a foothold in Europe and have a mail order business all year around." (It's the largest-selling dry packaged chili in the world.)

What is the fascination of chili cookoffs?

"It's just to meet people you like and have fun and drink beer and enjoy those who like what you like. . . ."

Observed
details are
important
here

Caliente Chili in Austin is just another side of the "my secret recipe" con. Their company offices are in an old, restored grain elevator near Austin's downtown. The office looks like a Wells Fargo station vintage 1880. There are two antique barber chairs, an antique pool table, antlers on the walls, old photos of chiliheads, a test kitchen on one side of the office and a constant smell of chili powder. Old fashioned. Homey. "We're all country here," Shorty Fry says, "Tom Nall, our vice president used to be a (rodeo) bull rider. . . ."

Another
key: a
"behind the
scenes"
glimpse is
important

Just old country folks playin' with their *bidness* (as Texans sometimes pronounce it). But behind one door is the heart of the operation—a glowing computer with a video-display screen, automatic warehousing, automatic orders and inventory, sales records, shipping, processing, humming away. It would make a Sears distribution center look shabby.

"I told the president last year we'd need a computer soon," Fry says. "He told me that it'd ruin the company image. I told him I'd build an outhouse around it if he liked. . . ." So Shorty Fry has her computer tucked away, sending out Two-Alarm Chili throughout the known world, while the good ole boys shoot pool and bullshit in the front offices. . . .

A quotation
end: But do
you believe
him or is
this another
chili con?

The winner at the Chiliympiad this year? It was Bob Ritchey of Garland, Texas, cooking "Contrary to Ordinary Chili." His secret recipe? No secret at all. "I just took the recipe off the back of a chili can. . . ." (pp. 29–34)

The Wall Street Journal Structure

Editors at *The Wall Street Journal* have developed an interesting form during the past months and years; observant readers can find examples of it in almost every issue of *The Journal.*

This form is particularly suited to business or industrial topics, and to complicated issues that appeal to readers of *The Journal.*

In brief, the writers begin to develop a problem or story focusing on one individual or family for the *first two, three, or four paragraphs* of a story. Then, at a subhead, the article enlarges to concentrate on the same topic as it applies to an entire industry.

At the end of the article, the focus narrows and the end two, three, or four paragraphs are devoted again to one individual—the same individual who was shown at the beginning—or perhaps another. The end shows how the individual conquered (or didn't conquer) the problem shown in the core of the article.

This technique makes it relatively easy to simplify a complicated business or economic problem.

The editors and staffers call the first section of the article "the nut" for it is the crux of the story—how industrial pollution, for instance, affects one family. Then, how the governmental clean-up operations are working, then, at the end, how the family is forced to move because federal clean-up agencies are not efficient.

The Wall Street Journal formula essentially works like this:

Individual
(or family)
to
Group
to
Individual
(or family)

The formula could also be stated like this:

Simple
to
Complex
to
Simple

As opposed to the Diamond or News-magazine form, this form usually presents material entirely in the present, although it is possible to present the "historical background" of a problem in the beginning of the body of the story, under the brief beginning.

Whenever possible, the writers and editors attempt to make the beginning segment and the end segment match in size and scope, either citing the same individual in the beginning *and* the ending, or citing two similar individuals.

Name: *The Wall Street Journal* form.

Frequency of use: Seen in almost every issue of *The Wall Street Journal.* Form also adopted by other writers and other publications.

Advantages: Used to simplify complicated business, economic, governmental, or other topics.

Disadvantages: Not workable for 'front-page disaster" stories.

Advisory. This technique also works for a "debate"—either written or spoken—because you have used this three section format for (a) *premise* (b) *evidence* and (c) *conclusion.*

This is an ideal story from *The Wall Street Journal,* Schlesinger & Guiles, 1987) that shows how the writers and editors use this structure.

Article begins with
one individual or family

Article expands to discuss
problem at national level, or
throughout one industry

Article breaks with subhead
after beginning segment

Article continues with
even emphasis throughout

Article "narrows" again to
end with one individual or
family

Article breaks with subhead
before end segment. Beginning
and end usually match in length
(2–4 paragraphs each).

FIG. 2.3.   *The Wall Street Journal* structure

Struggling Back
Job Programs Help
Workers Get Rehired,
But Often at Less Pay

Cost of Retraining Plans Is
Too High for Some Firms;
Some People Won't Move

A Venture-Capital Idea Flops

By Jacob M. Schlesinger
And Melinda Grenier Guiles
The Wall Street Journal
January 16, 1987

Here: a 2-
paragraph
beginning
about Mary
C. McEnrue

After being laid off five years ago from General Motors Corp.'s
Chevrolet assembly plant in Flint, Mich., Mary C. McEnroe
landed a variety of jobs—from baby-sitting to driving vans—but
none of the paid well or lasted long. "I was doing nothing," she
says, "waiting for GM to call me back." It didn't.

But in 1984, she got a letter inviting her to the newly formed United Auto Workers—GM Human Resource Center. The center gave her a series of courses—from basic math to "self-awareness—and paid her $3,000 tuition at a barbering college. As a result, she now has "a skill I can take anywhere" and a job at Eklips Hair Designers that she never would have got without the help. But there's a catch: at age 30, she makes less than half what she did assembling pistons at age 23.

Many Such Programs

The article expands to national scope at this point

Ms. McEnrue's mixed fortunes mirror those of other blue-collar workers squeezed out of manufacturing jobs as American companies scramble to become more competitive. An increasing number of people are now covered by so-called safety-nets—job search, security and retraining programs that help them find new jobs after they are laid off.

Such programs are a growing priority in the U.S. President Reagan has recommended nearly tripling the amount of government funding available for them, and, earlier this week, a Labor Department task force proposed establishing a new federal dislocated-worker unit to administer expanded training and reemployment assistance. Programs already in existence have aided thousands of workers.

But for thousands of others, the nets have holes. The new jobs often pay less, require relocation or extensive retraining, and force some workers to start over when they should be planning for retirement.

Consider, for example, the job search center and federally supported vocational retraining program set up by B.F. Goodrich Co. last March in Miami, Okla. Foreign competition forced Goodrich to close the Miami plant, which employed 1,900 workers. The closest jobs listed at the center were "probably 70 to 80 miles out," says Clifford Whitehead, vice president of the disbanding United Rubber Workers Local 318. Some were as far away as Kansas City, Mo. and Nashville, Tenn.

Lower Wages

And wages in the new jobs were "a comedown" from Goodrich's approximately $15 an hour, adds Wendell Prentice, the local office manager of the Oklahoma state employment service. "Now, anything else is $5 or $6." The upshot: 1,100 of the workers are still in Miami and still unemployed. "The company really did make an effort," Mr. Whitehead says. "I can't fault them at all." But, he adds, "it just wasn't what our people needed."

Undoubtedly, job-security programs have helped "remove the threat hanging over workers' heads," says Donald F. Ephlin, a UAW vice president who heads the union's GM department. He adds that the UAW wants to strengthen these programs in contract talks this year with GM and Ford Motor Co. But, he adds, "the best job-security program in the world is not an acceptable alternative to . . . a well-paying job in an industry that is booming."

In the past, industrial booms reduced the need for job-security and retraining programs. Blue-collar layoffs were generally viewed as temporary responses to short-term or seasonal problems. Workers in a few industries, such as auto and steel, received supplemental income assistance to tide them over.

Continuing Job Losses

Times have changed. More than 2.7 million blue-collar workers have permanently lost their traditional jobs since January, 1981, according to the Bureau of Labor Statistics. Such losses are continuing as companies face increasing foreign competition, more sophisticated technology and the realization that only efficient concerns will survive. GM alone plans to eliminate at least 26,000 blue-collar jobs over the next three years as it closes or consolidates 11 plants.

The upheaval is persuading government, unions and companies to expand job-security programs. The UAW led the way for labor in its 1982 and 1984 contracts with an elaborate safety net consisting of no-layoff guarantees for some workers and retraining for others. Other industries, such as steel, rubber and communications, have adopted similar provisions. Communities help by searching for retraining funds and persuading healthy companies to create jobs. Congressional and administration officials have made aiding dislocated workers a top legislative priority.

Michael G. Utley has the ultimate employment security: He can't be laid off. His job has disappeared at GM's Delco Remy plant at Anderson, Ind., because of technological change, but since 1984 the UAW has signed contracts with the Big Three auto makers that put workers who lose their jobs for certain reasons into a "job bank." They get full wages and benefits and do odd jobs at the plant until a regular slot opens up.

Mr. Utley, 39, currently administers the payroll for the 650 people at the plant's job bank, but placing other job-bank workers has been a struggle. Some of his colleagues at the Anderson plant helped remodel Boy Scout camps; another works as a secretary for the local March of Dimes. A union official at GM's Saginaw, Mich., plant says it will have job-bank workers do yard work at the factory site. Ford workers in Saline, Mich., painted a local YMCA building.

Furthermore, the number of jobs that a company can guarantee is limited. The auto-company job banks cover only workers facing layoff because of automation, productivity improvements or out-sourcing—moving work outside the company, often to a non-union shop. They don't cover workers affected by changes in sales or market conditions—the vast majority of blue-collar employees threatened. Of the 26,000 hourly jobs to be eliminated by the GM plant closings, only "a very small percentage will be covered under the jobs program," says Donald G. Gardner, GM's general director of employment relations and job security. "I'd be surprised if the figure was as high as 10%."

Some GM workers could be offered jobs at other plants under contractual transfer provisions. Such provisions, which have been written into many labor agreements, have helped preserve jobs for some workers whose companies were laying off people in one location while hiring at others. Not all employees take advantage of such opportunities, however. Since 1982, for example, Ford has offered 18,000 laid-off workers the chance to work if they moved elsewhere. Almost 60% rejected it.

Staying Put

Joseph Szramka, a steering-linkage assembler in Buffalo, N.Y., until last April, has had offers to transfer to GM plants in Massachusetts and Pennsylvania. But his wife just had a baby, he owns his own home, and he doesn't want to move from the area in which he has lived for all his 31 years. "Just to pick up a family and leave is pretty hard to do," he says. So he is collecting unemployment benefits and searching for a local job—without much luck. "There are signs for help wanted at places like McDonald's," he says, "but I'm looking for something a little better."

Even if a worker is willing to move, his colleagues at the new location might want a neighbor to get the job. In 1985, the UAW local at American Motor Corp.'s Jeep plant in Toledo, Ohio, waged a bitter, though unsuccessful, court battle to prevent the transfer of 400 workers threatened with layoff from the company's Kenosha, Wis., assembly plant.

Moreover, transfer rights aren't much use when a company is slashing its entire work force. Partly as a result of this, programs that help people find jobs outside their company have become more widespread. Some retraining programs have had spectacular results. An A.G. Edwards brokerage office in Buffalo has promised to take up to five laid-off auto workers from the local UAW-GM Human Resource Center. One furloughed Ford worker used his tuition to become a baseball umpire. Another became a lawyer. Of the 113,600 workers who participated in federally financed programs in 1984 and completed their training by June, 1985, 65% had found jobs, according to a government study.

Despite these successes, job-search and retraining programs face a thicket of difficulties. Often such programs are a nightmare to administer, and ideas that sounded great in principle fall flat in practice. One innovative aspect of the 1984 GM-UAW contract was a $100 million venture-capital fund to help workers start new businesses. Not a penny has been spent so far; the company and the union have had difficulty generating interest in and defining the purpose of the fund.

Another problem is cost, which can be prohibitive for companies already trying to cut expenses. The placement cost for Buffalo industrial workers in a 1983 demonstration project averages $3,014 per person—partly because the project included expensive retraining. Job-search programs that offer classes in resume-writing and interviewing techniques—but no retraining—can be cheaper. When Dana Co., a Toledo-based maker of truck parts, closes a plant, it spends about $125 a person to provide such services to displaced hourly workers.

Because of the expense, companies and communities often seek government funds. However, Congress slashed the fiscal 1986 budget for Title 3 of the Job Training Partnership Act, the main federal program for displaced workers, to about $96 million from $223 million in fiscal 1985. The fiscal 1987 funding is slated to go back up to about $200 million. For fiscal 1988, President Reagan has proposed a new $980 million program that would combine Title 3 with other dislocated-worker programs.

Minnesota's Woes

However, that won't help Minnesota, which has barely enough in its current budget to cover one plant closing but faces shutdowns at a frozen-foods plant, a meat-packer, a toy manufacturer, a farm-machinery company and a building-supply firm. About 1,500 workers will be "left to fend for themselves," says Jeff Farmer, the Minnesota AFL-CIO coordinator of the programs.

Some job-program problems lie with the jobless themselves. "There are probably 25% that won't come no matter what you offer just because they can't see beyond their own anger and hostility to the company," says Frederick W. DeRoche, vice president of Arbor Consulting Group, Inc., a Plymouth, Mich., outplacement firm.

Another problem is poorly structured training. Sandra Riffle says she saw a robot only once in a 10-month, county-sponsored electronic/robotics course in 1982, shortly after being laid off from Michigan Bell in Pontiac, Mich. She says the 20 people in the class got plenty of technical training but never had any hands-on experience. "We could tell you what was a diode," she says, but she couldn't figure out "what was wrong with a TV." After the course, she took a job in a flea market.

Declining Pay

The most unsettling aspect of job search and retraining programs is that many workers who find stable jobs must sacrifice
their former standard of living. A recent federal study concluded
that earnings of workers displaced from durable-goods industries
fell an average of 21%, to $273 a week from $344.

The article | John Truszkowski, a 41-year-old father of three, feels the
narrows | pinch. After almost 20 years at Goodyear Tire & Rubber Co.'s
here, to a | Jackson, Mich., tire plant, he was laid off when it closed in 1984.
portrait of | Goodyear offered counseling on interviewing techniques and
another | resumes, but, he asks, "What kind of resume would I have,
individual, | graduating from high school and starting off in a shop in a rub-
to match | ber factory?" As for federally financed training programs, he
the opening | asks, "What do you do, quit a job to go to school, or do you
section | try to feed your family?"

For two years, he took odd jobs. Today, he is a route salesman
for a dairy, making half what he did at Goodyear. "I feel for-
tunate I've at least got a job," he says. (pp. 1, 8)

Modified Forms

In some cases, the writer may modify one of these forms because the material
suggests a combined approach. Traditionally the easiest form to modify is
the Diamond or News-magazine structure.

Writing in *The Texas Observer* freelancer Montgomery Cottier (1981) used
a modified structure in his investigative article, "Thanks of a Grateful Nation," about abuses in the VA hospital complex in Waco, Texas.

Notice Cottier's descriptive beginning, with the interesting phrase: "He had
the longtime inmate's ingrained habit of sitting, hunched over, legs crossed
at the knees and back curled up and self-contained. He eyes continuously
roamed, darted, never quite at rest."

And later in the beginning, Cottier used an interesting twist on the old
cliché "the squeaking wheel gets the grease."

At the first spacebreak, Cottier began a *diary* form, showing on a
chronological basis, how the story unfolded. Notice how many paragraphs
begin with a diary or date form:

- It was Aug. 28, 1978. . . .
- After the third incident, in September, 1978. . . .
- Later that day. . . .
- "About two or three weeks later. . . ."
- About a week later. . . .

- On November 20, 1978. . . .
- In February, 1979. . . .
- Kelly's report was completed and released to the public in June, 1980. . . .

Thanks of a Grateful Nation
by Montgomery Cottier
The Texas Observer

Cottier uses
a fine
descriptive
beginning

Alvin D. Slaton was a 46-year-old ex-convict in 1978, a tall, fleshy man with a string of convictions on his record ranging from armed robbery to murder. He had the longtime inmate's ingrained habit of sitting, legs crossed at the knees and back hunched over, curled up and self-contained. His eyes continuously roamed, darted, never quite at rest.

Al Slaton, a newly-hired nurse's aide assigned to train at Building 91 of the Waco Veteran's Administration Medical Facility, also had the longtime convict's inner sense that this time he's better not louse up. Time was slipping steadily away, and new starts didn't come as easily at 46 as they had at 20 or 30.

A nice
twist on an
old cliché

To Slaton, one of the most important elements of not messing up, of getting along on the job, was not making waves. They taught you a lot about that in prison, and, if you lived, you learned that while it was true that the squeaky wheel is the one that received attention, the scrap yards are full of the remains of wheels which squeaked once too often.

He uses a
well-crafted
summary to
end this
section

But there was something inside Slaton which made it impossible for him to watch indifferently an all-to-frequent occurrence: employees of the V.A. hospital—the place that Slaton had come to for steady, respectable employment, a haven from his past and its casual brutality—were beating patients. As a result of watching those beatings and trying to stop them, Slaton initiated a major investigation at the V.A. hospital in Waco, an investigation which revealed the kind of horror stories which come from too many veteran's facilities. It is a story with a beginning and a middle, but no ending.

*   *   *

Diary form
begins here

"I was less than a week on the job," Slaton recalls, "training on Building 91, when the first incident occurred."

It was Aug. 28, 1978. An ordinary day, with what to everyone but Slaton were ordinary events. An elderly man, long confined to a wheelchair, bound by cloth restraints during the day and tied to his mattress at night, periodically began to writhe and pull at his confinings, trying once again to rise on legs that would never again carry him.

Slaton wondered how the staff would cope with the matter.

He soon found out.

One of the nurse's aides, distracted from the almost endless paperwork, strode up to the man and delivered a good swift blow to his head. The struggling and writhing stopped.

"I felt that blow," says Slaton. "I was beaten in prison, and I was knocked around and hung from the wall by handcuffs on my wrists." Slaton's wrists bear deep scars, not across the insides but across the backs of the wrists, where the weight of the man's body would have caused cuffs to dig in and finally cut the flesh.

"There was nothing I could do about it in prison," Slaton adds. "But this was different. The only crime this old patient had committed was to become sick and feeble, and he was in this hospital because somewhere along the line he had served his country."

Later, two more acts of violence against the old man occurred.

Chronology continues
After the third incident, in September, 1978, Slaton was transferred from Building 91 to Building 92. Like many of the other buildings at the sprawling V.A. hospital, built in 1932 and oriented primarily toward psychiatric care, Building 92 is a large brick structure housing psychiatric patients behind heavy doors and windows dimmed by thick steel mesh. Some 1,400 staff members, operating on a budget of $2 million annually, handle approximately 1,900 outpatient visits each year. A few days after Slaton's transfer, he approached his instructor, Ann Davidson, R.N. and told her of the beatings he had witnessed in the old building. She suggested that Slaton report the matter to Faye M. Roach, associate chief of nursing, as specified in the official hospital policy manual.

Later that day, Slaton saw Roach. After listening to his story, she called Chief of Nursing Services Mary Haynie, and told her that Slaton was sitting in her office and would like to make a patient abuse report. Mrs. Roach told Slaton that Haynie would be in touch with him.

"About two or three weeks later," according to Slaton's affidavit in the subsequent V.A. investigation, "I saw Faye Roach in the hospital canteen and she asked me what had ever happened on the abuse report. I told her I didn't know, as I had heard nothing more about it. She then asked me if Nurse Haynie had ever talked to me and I said no, and she commented that she had done all she could."

About a week later, Slaton was transferred to Building 90, another psychiatric ward. Slaton noticed that all the doors on the ward were locked, and that patients were denied access to water fountains and restrooms.

When he questioned the locked door policy, Slaton was told that the doors were locked on orders from Head Nurse Doris Harper, who reportedly didn't want patients wandering out into the hallway, where they might be seen by visitors. According to one of the orderlies with whom Slaton discussed the matter, Nurse Harper felt that such contact would not be good for the patients.

As a result of the locked door policy, Slaton noticed, the patients received liquids only with their meals, and, denied access to the restrooms, frequently urinated and defecated on the floors.

Slaton questioned Nurse Harper about the locked door policy and was told that, contrary to what other staff members had said, she had given explicit orders for the doors to remain open. "After that," he said, "I started unlocking the doors every time I was on duty."

Other problems weren't so easily solved.

*   *   *

Key date
highlights
new section

On November 20, 1978, a nursing aide on Ward 90-A North discovered that Luther Rollins, an elderly patient, had urinated and defecated while tied to his mattress. Although the infraction was common among patients who, old and thoroughly disoriented, found themselves bound securely to their mattresses at the onset of nature's call, the nursing aide began working the elderly man over, paying special attention to the chest and abdomen, where, Slaton noted, "bruises from the blows wouldn't show."

In addition, Slaton reported seeing patients Richard Ford, Oscar Hartley and Frank Priestly suffer physical abuse from some of the nursing aides working on the ward.

Remembering the lack of response to his first report, Slaton did not go to his supervisors with the Rollins beating. "I knew something had to be done," he later told investigators looking into the matter, "but I didn't know how to go about it."

He made one more try through the Waco V.A. administration, telling Mike Bays, personnel assistant to the nursing administrator on the three wards. On Dec. 5, 1978, Hays and Slaton called on Nurse Haynie, repeating Slaton's original report and adding the incidents he had since observed. "Once again," Slaton said, "nothing happened."

Investigation

Having followed the approved hospital policy procedures to their limit, and, in the case of contacting personnel assistant Bays, having exceeded them, without visible results, Slaton was faced with a particularly nasty decision.

On the one hand, he had done all that was required of him in reporting the instances of patient abuse, to do more might smack of insubordination. On the other hand, the patients were still being handled from day to day by the staff members who beat, kicked, insulted and abused them.

In February, 1979, Waco V.A. Administrator Jerry Brannon was sent a letter signed by "A Concerned Nurse," detailing several instances of patient abuse in Building 90, and noting that, "it's no secret that patients have been slapped, kicked, beaten and burned by certain employees . . . the bruises, black marks and broken limbs are often inflicted by certain sadistic employees. No man can have 25 bruise marks on his body without something being maliciously wrong."

Although the letter was written to appear as though its author was a young married female nurse, it was written by Slaton. He confirmed the fact in an interview in the Waco *Tribune-Herald* on June 13, 1980. (Slaton said he masked his identity in the letter because he had been worried about the security of his job. He remained anonymous until his year's probation was up, by which time enough attention had been drawn to the abuse cases so that his wouldn't seem the act of a disgruntled employee.)

Copies of the letter were also sent to the V.A. in Washington and to several congressmen. (Brannon denied ever receiving his copy.) On the basis of the letter, a field audit team was sent to Waco from the V.A. regional headquarters in Atlanta in July, 1979. The results of the audit led V.A. officials to send, within three months, a full investigating team headed by Special Investigator Russell Kelly. Kelly conducted a four-month investigation of the Waco facility, finishing in February, 1980. Virtually everything in Slaton's letter was found to be true.

During the investigation, two of the principals left the scene. Citing reasons of health, hospital administrator Brannon announced his retirement, effective Feb. 29, 1980. Before he left, however, Brannon talked with Special Investigator Kelly and his assistants, Karen Hawkins and John Swatling, who felt the conversation important enough to record in their report on the investigation. Brannon told the trio from the V.A. Inspector General's office that the troubles at his hospital were the result of a conspiracy among black employees and "some white employees, to discredit the current chief of nursing services, Ms. Haynie, and thereby discredit the chief of staff, Dr. Aaron Longfield." Brannon also complained that information concerning patient abuse was routinely kept from him until the investigation. "In an obvious attempt to discredit me, as well."

Another employee chose to retire at about the same time. The nursing aide whose treatment of patient Luther Rollins had sparked the initial hue and cry also left, citing reasons of health—without, however, making extensive comments to the investigators. No action has been taken against him.

Following the retirements, but before the release of Kelly's investigative report, assistant hospital director Melvin Baker commented, "We don't expect too many changes around here as a result of the investigation, because we feel that we've pretty much plugged all the holes."

                              *   *   *

Again, a
date is used
to begin a
new section

Kelly's report was completed and released to the public in June, 1980. It stated that "patients on Ward 90-A North (were) routinely cuffed, pushed, and spoken to harshly on a daily basis" and confirmed Slaton's reports of violence against patients.

In the meantime, relatives of abused patients, both those on Ward 90-A North and those in other buildings, began calling and writing Slaton and the handful of reporters working on the story.

Of the dozen or so letters, most resembled the story of Mrs. Luther Rollins of Gustine, a small town in Comanche County. Mrs. Rollins said she was called by a social worker at the Waco V.A. and told that her husband was going to require surgery for a ruptured bladder. The social worker reported that there were two conflicting stories concerning the cause of the injury. Mrs. Rollins never learned what really happened.

Other relatives had similar stories of sudden injuries and even deaths.

Mrs. Almeda Hubbard of Houston questioned the report that her brother Lawrence Joines, had sustained a broken hip when he took a swing at an orderly. Shortly after complaining, Mrs. Hubbard was informed that her brother, a virtually comatose and bedridden man who had been a patient for 36 years, was due to be discharged, and that she had 30 days to find a place for him.

Mrs. Hubbard eventually succeeded in getting the discharge order rescinded.

Mrs. Melvin E. Smith of Fort Worth wrote Slaton that she was still upset over the August 1978 death of her brother, Claude T. Miller Jr., who reportedly died of cardiac arrest. But Mrs. Smith learned, "he was badly bruised, and the autopsy report . . . said his lungs, liver and kidneys were gorged with blood."

Getting Better

In Washington Veterans Administration headquarters, Kelly's report along with a confirmed instance of patient abuse at the Marlin, Tex. V.A. hospital last June, has led top level administrators to call for increased vigilance by hospital employees against patient mistreatment.

With the retirement of one employee implicated in the patient abuse investigation, and the recent resignation of another, Slaton said he felt that "a warning has been made to the employees who can't control themselves when working with the patients."

And, more importantly, he added, the employees who are genuinely concerned about the patients' welfare "now know that there is something they can do about it."

Things have changed considerably on Ward 90, for example, since the visit of Russell Kelly and his investigating team. Doors once bolted are now open, patients have access to water fountains and restrooms, doctors and administrators who used to make rare appearances now frequent the building and the ward has become something of a showplace.

And Slaton? After the Kelly investigation was completed, Slaton transferred from the Waco hospital to the Temple V.A. facility, which deals chiefly with medical and surgical cases.

After he claimed authorship of the anonymous letter, Slaton was made the subject of a memo from the new Waco hospital director, Irvin D. Noll, who said that "our position has always been that the conditions described have never existed at Waco," and he added "we wonder if the writer was primarily concerned about the patient."

Cottier uses a Quote end—full of irony

In discussing the reaction from his former Waco superiors to his activities on behalf of the patients, Al once commented, "It's hardly what you'd call the thanks of a grateful nation." (pp. 15, 22–24)

14 Types of Effective Endings

In the Inverted Pyramid style, the story just "dribbles down the page" and when the writer runs out of facts, data, and material, the story ends. The ending in the Inverted Pyramid material is really not an ending at all. The story simply stops.

But in the Diamond or News-magazine form and in *The Wall Street Journal* form and even in a Modified Form story, *the ending should have impact.*

If the beginning has impact, in a Diamond form or *Wall Street Journal* of Modified form story, *the ending should have just as much impact.*

It should not surprise you to discover that just as there are certain categories of beginnings, there are also specific *categories of endings.*

The endings of stories—except for the Inverted Pyramid style—have exactly the same purpose as beginnings—to impress the reader:

- To make the reader "hear" again the subject of the story, with a good quotation at the end;
- To make the reader think about the subject of a personality portrait or profile with an anecdote at the end.
- To make the reader think about the subject with a question at the end.
- To make the reader "hear again" the writer of the story, with an "I" ending;
- To make the reader think of the *future* of the subject.
- To end the story with emphasis, with an emotional impact ending.

Although there are not as many categories of endings as beginning—some beginnings are too complicated to use as endings and some simply do not lend themselves to endings, here are *14 categories of endings, which are all effective, all easy to use, and all generally appropriate* for most story types.

THE SUMMARY ENDING

"Now all Isiah has to do"

This is the equivalent of the summary beginning, but could also be called the "storybook ending" for it is like the old children's storybooks that ended "And everybody lived happily ever after. The End." The writer simply wraps up the subject and ends the article with an appropriate conclusion.

In *Sports Illustrated*, staff writer William Nack (1987) profiled pro basketball star Isiah Thomas in an article headlined " 'I Have Got To Do Right,' " a quote from Thomas. The subhead for the article said "Up from mean streets, Piston hero Isiah Thomas ushers in a new era for his family."

Nack's ending:

> Now all Isiah has to do is somehow, someday, lead the Pistons to a world title—a goal that does not seem all that farfetched these days. After a period of adjusting to major personnel changes—Detroit acquired the high-scoring Adrian Dantley for Kelly Tripucka in one of the biggest deals of the off-season—the Pistons went on a tear that has made them one of the hottest teams in the NBA. With Dantley and Thomas providing a potent one-two punch, Detroit won 18 out of 22 games and was suddenly being taken seriously as a playoff contender. "That's the only reason that you play and practice," Thomas says. "If I work hard enough, we'll win it. If our team doesn't win a championship while I'm here, I wasn't good enough to win it. It's that simple."
>
> Yes, simple, just as basketball is a simple game, a children's game. What Isiah Thomas has to decide now is whether he wants to gear up or gear down, whether he wants to razzle and dazzle or squeeze and ease—whether he just wants to play, or wants to win. The question is really as simple as the game itself, and as old as Naismith. (p. 73)

Name: Summary ending.

Frequency of use: Often seen.

Length: Varies with material.

Difficulty range: 3–5. Generally easy method to use.

THE DESCRIPTION ENDING

"It kept struggling in an elementary fury"

The editors of *The Best of Pulitzer Prize News Writing* (Sloan, McCrary, & Cleary, 1986) state:

> Though decades have familiarized the world's people with the effect of the atomic bomb, William Laurence's article on the bombing of Nagasaki, Japan, still leaves the reader awestruck. The concrete detail of the narrative helps the reader live the experience of being on the bombing mission, feeling the drama and tension as the bomber nears its target, with each paragraph building the anticipation of the devastation that ultimately will occur. Laurence's description of the explosion leaves the reader with the indelible picture of a monumental fury. (p. 32)

William Laurence won the Pulitzer Prize for Reporting in 1946 for his article, "Atomic Bombing of Nagasaki told by Flight Member." It appeared in *The New York Times,* September 9, 1945.

He used a descriptive ending, without any additional commentary. Here are the last 10 paragraphs of his article:

> Out of the belly of *The Great Artiste* what looked like a black object went downward.
>
> Captain Bock swung around to get out of range: but even though we were turning away in the opposite direction, and despite the fact that it was broad daylight in our cabin, all of us became aware of a giant flash that broke through the dark barrier of our arc welder's lenses and flooded our cabin with intense light.
>
> We removed our glasses after the first flash, but the light still lingered on, a blueish-green light that illuminated the entire sky all around. A tremendous blast wave struck our ship and made it tremble from nose to tail. This was followed by four more blasts in rapid succession, each resounding like the boom of cannon fire hitting our plane from all directions.
>
> Observers in the tail of our ship saw a giant ball of fire arise as though from the bowels of the earth, belching forth enormous white smoke rings. Next they saw a giant pillar of purple fire, ten thousand feet high, shooting skyward with enormous speed.
>
> By the time our ship had made another turn in the direction of the atomic explosion the pillar of purple fire had reached the level of our altitude. Only about forty-five seconds had passed. Awe-struck, we watched it shoot upward like a meteor coming from the earth instead of from outer space, becoming even more alive as it climbed skyward through the white clouds. It was no longer smoke, or dust, or even a cloud of fire. It was a living thing, a new species of being, born right before our incredulous eyes.
>
> At one stage of its evolution, covering millions of years in terms of seconds, the entity assumed the form of a giant totem pole, with its base about three

miles long, tapering off to about a mile at the top. Its bottom was brown, its center was amber, its top white. But it was a living totem pole, carved with many grotesque masks grimacing at the earth.

Then, just when it appeared as though the thing had settled down into a state of permanence, there came shooting out of the top a giant mushroom that increased the height of the pillar to a total of forty-five thousand feet. The mushroom top was even more alive than the pillar, seething and boiling in a white fury of creamy foam, sizzling upward and then descending earthward, a thousand Old Faithful geysers rolled into one.

It kept struggling in an elemental fury, like a creature in the act of breaking the bonds that held it down. In a few seconds it had freed itself from its gigantic stem and floated upward with tremendous speed, its momentum carrying it into the stratosphere to a height of about sixty thousand feet.

But no sooner did this happen when another giant mushroom, smaller in size than the first one, began emerging out of the pillar. It was as though the decapitated monster was growing a new head.

As the first mushroom floated off into the blue it changed its shape into a flowerlike form, its giant petals curving downward, creamy white outside, rose-colored inside. It still retained that shape when we last gazed at it from a distance of about two hundred miles. The boiling pillar of many colors could also be seen at that distance, a giant mountain of jumbled rainbows, in travail. Much living substance had gone into those rainbows. The quivering top of the pillar was protruding to a great height through the white clouds, giving the appearance of a monstrous prehistoric creature with a ruff around its neck, a fleecy ruff extending in all directions, as far as the eye could see. (pp. 1, 35)

Your descriptive endings may not be as dramatic as that, but they should be as vivid as possible to show your readers what you saw.

Name: Descriptive ending.

Length: Varies with material.

Frequency of use: Seen occasionally.

Difficulty range: 7–10.

THE ANECDOTE ENDING

"Why Noah, I'm surprised!"

Just as many personality profiles can effectively begin with an anecdote, or a true story that shows character or personality, so too, can the same profile story end with an anecdote, to re-emphasize the character or personality of the profile's subject.

These end anecdotes do not have to be lengthy to be effective.

Here, from *Parade* magazine, is one segment from a historical profile of Noah Webster. Written by Diane Ackerman (1987), the story's subtitle and title were:

How Noah Webster helped shape the nation
He put Words in Our Mouths

Ackerman detailed how Webster helped unify the young nation. His *Blue Book Speller* eventually sold 100 million copies. She wrote:

> In his long lifetime (he died in 1843 at age 84), Webster published many other textbooks and wrote about history, economics, geography, politics, linguistics and medicine. He edited two newspapers. He fathered the copyright laws. He helped found Amherst College. He mastered 20 languages. He practiced law. But his greatest achievement, the one that wears his name, is the dictionary he spent 20 years compiling. There have been eight editions (the most recent with 470,000 words) in a series dating back to 1828, each one attended by enormous controversy, since new words may appear that seem trendy to some, while older words suddenly disappear like great uncles or aunts we rarely saw but were fond of. (p. 12)

Writer Ackerman stressed throughout the article how Webster was obsessed with using the right word in the right context. Her end anecdote:

> Formal portraits of Webster as an adult show a sour-faced man with hooded brown eyes and upswept hair. Those who knew him said he was pompous and austere, a tightwad who prized industry above all. There are many legends about him but my favorite recalls when his wife caught him kissing the chambermaid. "Why, Noah I'm surprised!" she is supposed to have said. To which he replied, like the bona fide schoolmaster he was, "Madame, *you* are astonished; *I* am surprised." (p. 14)

Name: Anecdote ending.

Frequency of use: Occasionally seen.

Length: Varies with material.

Difficulty range: 3–4. Generally easy to use.

Advisory. An especially effective ending to use with a personality portrait or profile article.

THE FIRST-PERSON "I" ENDING

"I peered over the edge and breathed slowly"

Just as the writer can "talk to" the reader using the first-person "I" form in the beginning of the article, so too, can the writer end a story with the "I."
Writing for *The New York Times* News Service, Clifford D. May (1986)

used the first-person "I" throughout an article about skiing Corbet's Couloir, in Jackson Hole, Wyoming. His lead:

> JACKSON HOLE, Wyo.—One thing about a new ski season: it provides sharp perspective on the passage of time.
>
> Though the size of the mountains and the pitch of the trails remain constant, the response of the skier's mind and muscles is bound to vary as the years slip by.
>
> This thought struck me forcefully on a visit to Jackson Hole, Wyo., after being too long away from the slopes. I was standing at the top of Corbet's Couloir, a run that is to Western skiers something akin to what Jesse James must have been to frontier sheriffs.
>
> To negotiate Corbet's requires that one slide off a precipice directly into space, fall roughly 15 feet, depending on recent snowfall accumulations, and begin carving precise turns immediately upon touching down on the nightmarishly steep snake of snow that uncoils between two sheer walls of weathered rock. Those who fail can expect to face disgrace, humiliation and, likely as not, an assortment of orthopedic complications. (sec. 10, p. 18)

His end:

> Before leaving Jackson Hole, I returned to Corbet's Couloir one more time. I knew I could manage the trail. It was just a matter of preparing myself psychologically.
>
> I peered over the edge and breathed slowly. Then it occurred to me that maybe I had been misinformed. Maybe some mountains and trails do indeed become steeper with the passage of time. (sec. 10, p. 18)

Name: First-person "I" ending.

Frequency of use: Seen occasionally.

Length: Varies with subject.

Difficulty range: 5–7. Not particularly difficult if writer has mastered the first-person "I" problems inherent in the complete story.

Advisory. Especially appropriate matched with the first-person "I" beginning.

THE SECOND-PERSON "YOU" ENDING

"You could buy a bronze model"

If you speak to the reader with the "you" beginning, it is just as effective to also end speaking to the reader.

The reader puts down your work with your voice in his or her "inner ear."

The February 1986 issue of *Better Homes and Gardens,* contained Michael Leccese's article, "Historic House Update: Is the National Register for You?" His beginning was:

> You just bought a 1921 Georgian Revival house out in the country. Although the house features fanlight windows, gravity-defying curved staircases, and multipatterned brick, it never struck you as particularly historic. That honor is reserved for southern plantations, Newport mansions, and 17th-century New England cottages. Right?
>
> Not necessarily. An intact structure of architectural or historical importance can make the federal government's National Register of Historic Places, administered by the U.S. Department of the Interior, through the National Park Service. Among 37,491 listings accrued since its creation in 1966, the register includes Indian burial mounds, 19th century office buildings, entire row-house neighborhoods, and even the 399-foot-high launch tower from the Apollo 11 moon shot.

The article described how you can apply to have your house listed in the National Register.

Leccese's ending:

> A register listing will not automatically qualify you for lucrative investment tax credits for rehabilitation. That 25 percent tax write-off applies only to commercial properties such as apartment houses, offices, and factories. A historic-house owner carving out new apartments in a basement or loft might qualify, however. Again ask your SHPO.
>
> Finally, there are a couple of misconceptions to clear up. First, National Register listing does not grant some historic-preservation official the right to tell you what to do with your house. You can raze it for a miniature golf course, if local zoning permits. Second, the government will not give you a plaque. You can buy a bronze model, however, for about $140.

Name: Second-person "you" ending.

Frequency of use: Often seen.

Length: varies with subject.

Difficulty range: 1–3. Relatively easy to use.

Advisory. Particularly effective coupled with a "you" beginning.

THE QUOTATION ENDING

"After all, tomorrow is another day"

Here the writer ends with a good quotation, which can be either the principle personality in the story, *or* a significant quotation from another personality associated with the subject.

One of the most famous endings in literature is the quotation from Margaret Mitchell's *Gone With the Wind*:

> With the spirit of her people who would not know defeat, even when it stared them in the face, she raised her chin. She could get Rhett back. She knew she could. There had never been a man she couldn't get, once she set her mind upon him.
>
> "I'll think of it all tomorrow, at Tara. I can stand it then. Tomorrow, I'll think of some way to get him back. After all, tomorrow is another day." (p. 1037)

Here is the end of an article about war and war films, by Desmond Ryan (1987) of the Knight-Ridder News Service. the article appeared in *The Fort-Worth Star-Telegram* under the title:

War as Reality
Hollywood's combat movies
take us to hell
but don't bring us back

The end of Ryan's article was:

> *Platoon* is a great American film that was a long time coming—and perhaps it could not be otherwise with this tragic war. But it is as timely as ever.
>
> As Ron Kovic, the paralyzed Vietnam veteran who wrote *Born on the Fourth of July* once said, "The war's not over. The war is between those of us who caught hell and those who gave it out. Just because it's not on TV doesn't mean they stopped giving it out. Ask someone who's fought one. They'll tell you a war isn't over until you don't have to live with it anymore." (p. D1)

Name: Quotation ending.

Length: Varies with material.

Frequency of use: Often seen in books, newspapers, and magazines.

Difficulty range: 1–3. Usually easy to use.

Advisory. The quotation ending is probably the most effective and most empathetic ending that can be used.

THE QUESTION ENDING

"Ever fallen in a steep, snow-covered hill?"

A logical, meaningful question can be asked at the beginning of your article, to pull the reader into the article. The same can be done at the end of the article; you can ask a question *to keep your reader thinking about the article.*

The same rules apply to the end question as to the beginning question: The reader should be capable, from the context of the story, to answer the question with a yes or no, or multiple choice, or the question should be clear and logical, if it is rhetorical in nature.

Carol Barrington (1987), writing in the *Fort Worth Star-Telegram,* used a question ending in an article "Cutting costs on the slopes? Best bet is going early," about cut-rate ski vacations. Her ending:

> No matter when and where you ski, you can cut lift costs by buying a multi-day ticket. One word of warning, however: do not commit to more than three, preferably non-consecutive days at a time; the savings is not worth the gamble on the weather.
>
> That's the voice of experience speaking. Several years ago a dense snow storm caught our family of five with prepaid lift tickets on the last day of a week-long ski trip—a potential loss of more than $75 if we decided to sit out the storm. The resort refused to close or refund our money. Instead, they issued huge plastic garbage bags, cut head and arm holes in appropriate places, and wrapped each of us around the waist with tape. Ever fallen on a steep, snow-covered hill wrapped in a full-length baggie? It makes strapping on the boards a whole new sport. (p. 8E)

Name: Question ending.

Frequency of use: Seen occasionally.

Length: Varies with subject.

Difficulty range: 3–4. Like the question beginning, relatively easy, if the writer remembers to ask a question that is understandable.

THE PARODY ENDING

"Dragnet is . . . dumb-de-dumb-dumb"

Occasionally a writer can add "a stinger" to the end of an article—a parody ending that can be particularly effective to end a review of a book, film, or play. This can be just as effective as the parody beginning, even more so. Unfortunately, just as the parody beginning may escape your imagination when working on a deadline, so too the perfect parody ending may occur to you several hours or several days after you had to finish the project.

Here, *Austin American Statesman* staff critic Kevin Phinney (1988) used such an ending in an entirely negative review of the film *Beetlejuice,* starring Michael Keaton.

> Jeffrey Jones, who was so wonderful as the Emperor in *Amadeus,* replays his role as the principal in *Ferris Bueller's Day Off,* and cameos from Robert Goulet and Dick Cavett are pointless.

Keaton is doing another movie altogether, and admittedly, his demonic antics are riveting. If there had been either a respectable ensemble performing alongside him or a plot as delicious as his delivery, the film might have had some zing. As it is, a day without *Beetlejuice* is like a day without a root canal. (p. C8)

The Austin Chronicle staff reviewer Kathleen Maher (1987) used the same technique with an equally devastating parody ending, using the famous Dragnet "theme" in a negative review of the film *Dragnet,* with Dan Ackroyd and Tom Hanks. The end was:

The first time director (Tom) Mankiewicz does not display any notable talent for comedy here; the camera always seems to be just a little late on the scene or too predictable. There's also the problem of inconsistency, as in the scene of a bad guy rally with Riefenstahlian overtones—it's just too much (not to mention the fact that it's already been done to death in *The Jewel of the Nile, Raiders of the Lost Ark* etc.). This particular problem should probably be laid at Ackroyd's door as well, because this kind of wild inconsistency also damaged *The Blues Brothers* and *Ghostbusters,* which he also co-wrote. It's partly a problem of too much money and too little restraint, but most of all of missed opportunities, and finally, *Dragnet* is, if you'll pardon me, dumb-de-dumb-dumb. (p. 22)

Name: Parody ending.

Frequency of use: Rare.

Length: Usually brief—it's a punchline or pun.

Difficulty range: 7–10.

Advisory.   Writers should use a parody ending that is current enough so readers will know what is being parodied.

THE LITERARY REFERENCE ENDING

". . . the ones less traveled by . . ."

If a literary reference is uncommon at the *beginning* of a story, it is even more uncommon at the end. If a literary reference can be used at the end of a story, it will add a significant touch of sophistication to the story.

The reference can be direct or indirect.

Here, the editors of *Time* used a direct reference in a feature obituary on Harold Macmillan, former Prime Minister of England. Published in the

January 12, 1978 issue of *Time*. The obit's title was "A Leader for the Last Days of Empire." The end segment was:

> Macmillan was remarkable among his contemporaries for his great sense of camaraderie acquired as a soldier during the slaughter on the Somme in World War I. He was fond of quoting a stanza written by British Poet Hilaire Belloc that neatly summed up his credo:
>
> > *From quiet homes and first*
> > *beginning,*
> > *Out to the undiscovered ends,*
> > *There's nothing worth the wear of*
> > *winning,*
> > *But laughter and the love of*
> > *friends.* (p. 49)

The *indirect reference* can also be used: In *Yankee* magazine for January, 1987, the editors featured a "House for Sale" (distinctive New England properties for sale is a regular feature in the magazine) that once belonged to Robert Frost. The house, was located in Concord Corners, Vermont.

The end of the article quoted current owner, Mrs. Edith Wells:

> Mrs. Wells has lived in the house since she and her college-professor husband Harold decided to buy it one evening in 1965 when, as she puts it, there were "in a lovely sherry haze." They'd been summering in the area for many years. Now that Mr. Wells is gone and she's approaching 80 by herself, Mrs. Wells has decided to move into an apartment attached to her son's house in Danville, Vermont. "I'm going to miss Concord Corners, though," she told us as we were preparing to leave. "I like living where most of the roads have grass running down through the middle of them."
>
> As we drove back to Concord, stopping once again to look at Shadow Lake and the White Mountains, we decided that Mrs. Wells had summed up *everything* wonderful about Concord Corners with her simple observation. There *is* grass growing in the middle of Concord Corners roads—at least the ones less traveled by—and surely that *would* make all the difference.

(The reference is, of course, to Frost's famous poem "The Road Not Taken.")

Name: Literary reference ending.

Frequency of use: Relatively rare.

Length: Varies.

Difficulty range: 8–10. Relatively difficult to end most articles with a literary reference.

THE SIMILE OR METAPHOR ENDING

"So we beat on, boats against the current"

If it is relatively rare to *begin* a story with a simile or metaphor, it is even more rare to *end* a story with one.

The most famous metaphor ending in American literature is F. Scott Fitzgerald's end to *The Great Gatsby:*

> Gatsby believed in the green light, the orgiastic future that year by year recedes before us. It eluded us then, but that's no matter—tomorrow we will run faster, stretch out our arms farther. . . . And one fine morning—
> So we beat on, boats against the current, borne back ceaselessly into the past.

If Fitzgerald had wished to change the meter and cadence of the last paragraph, he might have made the phrase a simile:

> So we beat on, *like boats against the current,* borne back ceaselessly into the past.

But who would criticize the genius of Fitzgerald?

Name: Simile or metaphor ending.

Frequency of use: Rare.

Length: Varies.

Difficulty range: 9–10. Seldom easy to end any piece of writing with an exceptional simile or metaphor.

THE EDITORIAL ENDING

"There are no easy answers"

Occasionally, the writer may end the article with an editorial supporting a position taken previously in the text. The reader has the choice of agreeing or disagreeing with the author based on proof shown in the text.

In 1985, University of Texas historian Robert H. Abzug published *Inside the Vicious Heart: Americans and the Liberation of Nazi Concentration Camps*; a stunning history of how the Allies opened the Nazi concentration camps and what they found there. The ending of this book read:

> There are no easy answers to how we should deal with our post-liberation knowledge, for in the end we confront the mutually exclusive desires to remember

and forget. However, we should recognize there are no soldiers to push us back into the theater to face the facts. We must be our own soldiers, constantly on the look out for subtle evasion. We must recognize that if we feel helpless when facing the record of human depravity, there was always a point at which any particular scene of madness could have been stopped. (pp. 172–173)

Sportswriter Red Smith covered Joe Louis's last fight—against Rocky Marciano, Oct. 26, 1951. Louis lost. Writing in *The New York Herald Tribune,* Smith's column on the fight was titled "Night for Joe Louis." Smith's last three paragraphs were:

It is easy to say, and it will be said, that it wouldn't have been like this with the Louis of ten years ago. It isn't a surprisingly bright thing to say, though, because this isn't ten years ago. The Joe Louis of October 26, 1951, couldn't whip Rocky Marciano, and that's the only Joe Louis there was in the Garden. That one was going to lose on points in a dreary fight that would have left everything at loose ends. It would have been a clear victory for Marciano, but not conclusive. Joe might not have been convinced.

Then Rocky hit Joe a left hook and knocked him down. Then Rocky hit him another hook and knocked him out. A right to the neck knocked him out of the ring. And out of the fight business. The last wasn't necessary, but it was neat. It wrapped the package, neat and tidy.

An old man's dream ended. A young man's vision of the future opened wide. Young men have visions, old men have dreams. But the place for old men to dream is beside the fire.

Name: Editorial ending.

Frequency of use: Seen occasionally.

Length: Varies with material.

Difficulty range: 4–6.

Advisory. Most appropriate with editorial, column, bylined, or opinion material.

THE EMOTIONAL ENDING

"I am haunted by waters"

In this ending, the writer pulls at the reader's heart—to evoke tears of joy or sorrow, pangs of conscience, or tremors of guilt.

My favorite emotional ending is from Jack Evans' article "Teddy," printed earlier in this book:

As the sun slips out of sight, the boat's passengers open a case of champagne, and the group of friends and family toast Teddy's memory. Afterward, they cast 2½ dozen red and white carnations into the water.

In the distance, the city lights of Corpus Christi shine brightly on the horizon. For the last time, Teddy was returned home to the bay, where as a small boy he sat alongside his grandparents and fished away the afternoons of his childhood. (p. 1)

In his book, *The Log From The Sea of Cortez,* first published in 1951, John Steinbeck presented a long detailed portrait of his dear friend Ed Ricketts, in an introductory essay he titled "About Ed Ricketts." Ricketts had died in 1948, when his car was hit by a Southern Pacific train, in Cannery Row. His death had haunted Steinbeck and the portrait of Ricketts was Steinbeck's attempt to lay Ricketts' ghost to rest.

Here is the last of Steinbeck's essay:

There it is. That's all I can set down about Ed Ricketts. I don't know whether any clear picture has emerged. Thinking back and remembering has not done what I hoped it might. It has not laid the ghost.

The picture that remains is a haunting one. It is the time just before dust. I can see Ed finishing his work in the laboratory. He covers his instruments and puts his papers away. He rolls down the sleeves of his wool shirt and puts on his old brown coat. I see him go out and get into his beat-up car and slowly drive away in the evening.

I guess I'll have that with me all my life. (1971 Bantam paperback ed. p. lxiv)

Earlier, we cited the beginning of the story "A River Runs Through It," from Norman Maclean's book *A River Runs Through It and Other Stories.* Here is the ending from that story:

Now nearly all those I loved and did not understand when I was young are dead, but I still reach out for them.

Of course, now I am too old to be much of a fisherman, and now of course I usually fish the big waters alone, although some friends think I shouldn't. Like many fly fishermen in western Montana where the summer days are almost Arctic in length, I often do not start fishing until the cool of the evening. Then in the Arctic half-light of the canyon, all existence fades to a being with my soul and memories and the sounds of the Big Blackfoot River and a four-count rhythm and the hope that a big fish will rise.

Eventually, all things merge into one, and a river runs through it. The river was cut by the world's great flood and runs over rocks from the basement of time. On some of the rocks are timeless raindrops. Under the rocks are the words, and some of the words are theirs.

I am haunted by waters. (p. 104)

Name: Emotional ending.

Frequency of use: Seen occasionally.

Length: Varies with subject.

Difficulty range: 7–10. Usually difficult to conjure emotion in a brief ending.

Advisory.   In this ending, less is more. It is better, in most cases to *underwrite* the ending, rather than to beat the reader over the head with a psychological club.

THE "FUTURE" ENDING

"There will . . . be three generations of the Hill family on the river."

Some articles in the diamond form and *The Wall Street Journal* form do not end in the present, but rather give the readers a glimpse or an educated guess at the future. This might be called a "look ahead" end, because it gives the reader a *look ahead* at the future, which might be next month, next year, or the next century.

In an article, "Sentinel at Niagara Falls" (Fensch, 1978) about a Canadian named Wes Hill, I explained how Wes Hill's father and brothers had been guardians at Niagara Falls since the 1930s, taking personal responsibility to rescue victims about to be swept over the Falls or adrift in the river below the Falls. They were—and are—a remarkable family.

Here was the end segment:

> Wes Hill has been responsible for the rescue of at least fifty people, whose boats lost power and were drifting toward the Falls, or people who were drowning, or people somehow trapped either by the Falls or the river and the whirlpool. Like the men who first successfully climbed Mount Everest "because it was there," Wes Hill challenges the river and the falls because he is there when someone needs help.
>
> There will, eventually, be three generations of the Hill family on the river, as sentinels for the unlucky or the unwary. Wes Hill has been training his children. Son Douglas, now nineteen, has been helping with rescues and body recoveries since he was eleven; Hill's other sons, David, twelve and Dan, fourteen, have also helped, as has his daughter Diane, fifteen.
>
> "Dad always said he'd like the rescues on the Niagara to stay in the Hill family," Wes says, "and I'm sure they will." (p. 64)

Name: Future ending.

Frequency of use: Seen occasionally.

Length: Varies with subject.

Difficulty range: 2–4. Relatively easy, if material supports an educated guess or surmise about the future.

THE COMBINATION ENDING

"Ironies swirled around Gardner"

Just as various categories of beginnings can be combined, it is possible to combine various categories of *endings*. In many cases, simpler is better—a single type of ending may be more appropriate than a multiple-type ending. But a multiple ending *is* possible.

Here is the *beginning* of a book review by Richard Gilman in *The New York Times Book Review* July 20, 1986. The book reviewed was *Stillness and Shadows* by novelist John Gardner, published posthumously:

> When John Gardner died at 49 in a motorcycle accident in 1982, he left a reputation as an extraordinarily prolific and versatile writer: poetry, plays, opera librettos, essays, translations, fables, stories and novels issued from him as if from some literary conglomerate. Popular and critical opinion about Gardner's output, especially about the fiction, was sharply divided. For those who, like myself, thought him a novelist whose debilities considerably outweighed his strengths, the posthumous publication of these two pieces of fiction, "Stillness" and "Shadows," will come as a melancholy confirmation. (p. 11)

The *end* segment of his review contained a paragraph of contradictory paradoxes, followed by an editorial paragraph:

> Ironies swirled around Gardner. He raged against what he saw as the heresy of "texture over structure" in fiction, yet his own often lacked clear shape. He lyrically apostrophized fiction as "life-affirming," and "celebration" and "discovery," yet his was mostly eccentric, self-indulgent, full or random, crabbed polemics. His career had progressed fairly well by the time of "Grendel," an amusing *jeu d'espirit,* and afterward he could write decently in a mode of social observation: the first part of "Freddy's Book," for example, or scattered sequences of "The Sunlight Dialogues" and "Mickelsson's Ghosts."
>
> But he wasn't content with that and continually lunged after the "secrets" of existence. Clumsy, long-winded, self-deluded, the victim of his sillier admirers, he was far from being the shaggy giant, like Cervantes, Dostoyevsky or Faulkner, he seems to have thought himself. The sad truth is that he was an inconsolable aspirant after literary size and significance, a writer with a hundred maimed styles and so, finally, with none. (p. 12)

Name: Combination ending.

Frequency of use: relatively rare.

Length: Varies with subject.

Difficulty range: 8–10. Usually difficult to merge styles of endings.

INSTANT CHECKLIST FOR ENDINGS

Just as some specific beginnings are appropriate for some story *categories,* specific endings are also appropriate for the same reasons. Some endings *fit* certain categories much better than others. This is particularly true with the Diamond or News-magazine form and *The Wall Street Journal* structures.

If you are stuck while you are working *toward* an ending, this list may help you find the right ending for the story you have in progress.

Are you writing a story about yourself?
Consider:
- The quotation ending;
- The anecdote ending;
- The "I" form ending;
- The summary ending;
- Other appropriate endings.

Are you writing about another person?
Consider:
- The anecdotal ending;
- The quotation ending;
- The summary ending;
- Other appropriate endings.

Are you writing about an event?
Consider:
- The quotation ending;
- The anecdote ending;
- The summary ending;
- Other appropriate endings.

Are you writing about a trend or problem in society?
Consider:
- The quotation ending;
- The second-person "you" ending;
- The future ending;
- The editorial ending;
- The emotional ending;
- The summary ending;
- Other appropriate endings.

Are you writing an editorial or an essay?
Consider:
- The quotation ending;
- The literary ending;
- The second-person ending "you" ending;
- The editorial ending;
- The summary ending;
- Other appropriate endings.

Are you writing an article that will largely describe a location or a scene?
Consider:
- The quotation ending;
- The first-person "I" ending;
- The second-person "you" ending;
- The summary ending;
- Other appropriate endings.

Are you writing "self-help," "do-it-yourself," instructional, or educational material?
Consider:
- The second-person "you" ending;
- The first-person "I" ending;
- The quotation ending;
- The summary ending;
- Other appropriate endings.

Are you writing psychological, religious, or motivational material?
Consider:
- The second-person "you" ending;
- The quotation ending;
- The question ending;
- The simile or metaphor ending;
- The first-person "I" ending;
- The editorial ending;
- The summary ending;
- The literary reference ending;
- Other appropriate endings.

Are you writing a book review, film review, or a dramatic review?
Consider:

- The quotation ending;
- The literary reference ending;
- The editorial ending;
- The summary ending;
- Other appropriate endings.

Are you writing a sports story?
Consider:
- The quotation ending;
- The anecdote ending;
- The summary ending;
- Other appropriate endings.

Are you writing an historical article?
Consider:
- The quotation ending;
- The anecdote ending;
- The summary ending;
- The future ending;
- The editorial ending;
- Other appropriate endings.

Selected Readings

Berner, R. T. (1986). Literary newswriting: The death of an oxymoron. *Journalism Monographs,* No. 99.

Clark, R. P. (1982, October). Plotting the first graph. *Washington Journalism Review.*

Clark, R. P. (1984, March). A new shape for news. *Washington Journalism Review.*

Fensch, T. (1984). *The hardest parts: Techniques for effective non-fiction.* Austin, TX: Lander Moore Books.

References

Abzug, R. (1985). *Inside the vicious heart: Americans and the liberation of nazi concentration camps.* New York and Oxford: Oxford University Press.

Ackerley, J. P. (1969). *My father and myself.* New York: Coward-McCann.

Ackerman, D. (1987, January 18). How Noah Webster helped shape the nation. *Parade,* pp. 12, 14.

Associated Press. (1985, May). [Feature article about drug-sniffing dog.]

Associated Press. (1986, December 31). [Profile of senior citizens in Springfield, MA.]

Associated Press. (1987, January). Education Department announces "Income Contingent Loan" plan.

Associated Press. (1987, January 16). 10 die as 2 planes collide over Salt Lake City.

Associated Press. (1987, Auust 14). Fast-food widow donates $1 million to democratic party.

Barrington, C. (1987, January 18). Cutting costs on the slopes? Best bet is going early. *The Fort Worth Star Telegram,* p. E8.

Bayles, M. (1986, December 12). An attorney's complaint. *The Wall Street Journal,* p. 15.

Beaver, C. (1987, January 11). Upwardly mobile. *The Daily Texan,* p. 10.

Bedard, P. (1987, September). DeSoto Adventurer II. *Car & Driver,* pp. 58–61.

Gohls, K. (1986, September 11). Fighting at home. *The Austin American Statesman,* p. D1.

Bombeck, E. (1988, April). [Column about the death of the mini-skirt.]

Bowen, E. (1987, February 2). Fateful decision on treating AIDS. *Time,* p. 62.

Capote, T. (1965). *In cold blood.* New York: Random House.

Capouya, J. (1986, December). John Wooden. *Sport,* p. 51.

Carroll, P. B. (1987, July 9). Landlubber reporter sails the Atlantic and survives, barely. *The Wall Street Journal,* p. 1.

Ceppos, R. (1987, February). Make the earth move. *Car & Driver,* p. 67.

Chicago Tribune News Service. (1987, January). [Article about sport as religion.]

Collins, D. (1987). [Feature about termite-hunting dogs.] Knight-Ridder News Service.

Cottier, N. (1981, February 27). Thanks of a grateful nation. *The Texas Observer,* pp. 15, 22–24.

Crews, F. (1980). *The Random House handbook.* New York: Random House.

Davis, J. T. (1986, October 16). A brush with art. *The Austin American Statesman,* p. D1.

Dent, J. (1986, November 14). Injury probably to end Dorsett's 1,000-yard run. *The Dallas Times Herald,* p. C1.

Dickens, C. *A tale of two cities.*

Dixon, J. (1987, January 2). Federal agent shot. *The Dallas Morning News,* p. 2.

Dorr, D. (1982). Profile of basketball player Mark Alcorn. *The St. Louis Post Dispatch.*

Evans, J. (1986, September 19). Teddy. *The Daily Texan,* Images sect. 1.

Fensch, T. (1978, May). Sentinel at Niagara Falls. *Cavalier,* pp. 60–64.

Fensch, T. (1983, April). Lookin' for a good bowl of red? *Cavalier,* pp. 29–33.

Fisher, D. (1983). *The war magician.* New York: Coward-McCann.

Fitzgerald, F. S. (1925). *The Great Gatsby.* New York: Scribner's.

Gernander, J. (1988). Conradt shoots for 500th victory Saturday. *The Daily Texan,* p. 1.

Gibson, W. (1966). *Tough, sweet and stuffy: An essay on modern American prose styles.* Bloomington, IN: Indiana University Press.

Gilman, R. (1986, July 7). Novelist in a mirror. *The New York Times Book Review,* p. 11.

Greene, J. (1987, January 4). Sports article about the Denver Broncos-New England Patriots football game. Knight-Ridder News Service.

Haas, A. (1984). *The doctor and the damned.* New York: St. Martin's Press.

Hacker, K. (1985, January). [Profile of Kevin Boyce.] Knight-Ridder News Service.

Hampton, W. (1986, November 12). Cotton race remains open. *The Daily Texan,* p. 13.

Hanley, D. (1988). Make no beans about chili.

Hansen, T. (1984, November 17). Volcano shores up history, beauty at park. *The Austin American Statesman,* TV Watch sect., p. 4.

Hanson, D. (1982). *The new alchemists: Silicon Valley and the micro-electronics revolution.* New York: Avon Books.

Holloway, D. (1987, January 7). Tough guys. *The Austin American Statesman,* p. D20.

Holmes, C. S. (1972). *The clocks of Columbus: The literary career of James Thurber.* New York: Atheneum.

House for sale. (1987, January). *Yankee* magazine.

Howe, A. (1986). When 10¢ equals $46,806 the IRS taxes a firm's patience. *The Philadelphia Inquirer.*

Hyer, M. (1987, December). Profile of Lesley Northrup. *The Washington Post* News Service.

Jabroslovsky, R. and Perry, J. M. (1984, October 8). New question in race: Is oldest U.S. president now showing his age? *The Wall Street Journal,* p. 1.

James, B. (1986, December). Casey Stengel. *Sport,* p. 85.

Jay, R. (1986). *Learned pigs and fireproof women.* New York: Villard Books.

Johnson, B. (1987). *The four days of courage: The untold story of the people who brought Marcos down.* New York: Free Press.

Kellman, M. (1987, September 2). Visions of Max Headroom. *The Chronicle of Higher Education,* p. B1.

Kelly, D. (1987, January 11). Closest thing to dyin' that I know of. *The New York Times Book Review,* p. 8.

Keteyian, A. (1986, December). How Julie Moss found ecstasy after losing to agony. *The San Diego Union.*

Kiester, E. Jr. (1986, December). Fever: New facts you should know. *Better Homes & Gardens.*

King, M. L. (1963, August 28). I have a dream. (Speech.)

Koepp, S. (1987, January 12). Hospitals learn the hard sell. *Time,* p. 56.

Kornheiser, T. (1986, December). Howard Cosell, *Sport,* pp. 59, 144.

Laurence, A. (1945, September 9). Atomic bombing of Nagasaki told by flight member. *The New York Times,* pp. 1, 35.

Leader for the last days of Empire. (1978, January 12). *Time,* p. 49.

Lecesse, M. (1986, February). Historic house update: Is the National Register for you? *Better Homes & Gardens.*

Lesser, W. (1985, October 20). Adultery with discussions. *The New York Times Book Review,* p. 14.

Lewis, S. (1927). *Elmer Gantry.* New York: Harcourt, Brace.

Liebling, A. J. (1961). *The Earl of Louisiana.* New York: Simon & Schuster.

Maclean, N. (1976). *A river runs through it and other stories.* Chicago: The University of Chicago Press.

Maher, K. (1987, July 10). [Review of the film *Dragnet.*] *The Austin Chronicle,* p. 22.

Manchester, W. (1978). *American Caesar: Douglas MacArthur, 1880–1964.* Boston: Little, Brown.

Mannix, Dan. (1950). *Step right up!* New York: Harper.

May, C. (1986, December 7). Sojourns in the snow: Hitting the heights at Jackson Hole. *The New York Times,* sec. 10, p. 18.

McGrady, M. (1986, December). Harrison Ford: Lucky, and patient, star. *Newsday.*

Melville, H. *Moby Dick.*

Metz, W. (1979). *Newswriting: From lead to "30"* (2nd rev. ed.). Englewood Cliffs, NJ: Prentice-Hall.

Meyer, S. (1986, January 29). Being there when friends are in need. *The Austin American Statesman.* Neighbor sect., p. 1.

Millier, A. (1939, July 2). Melancholy doodler. *The Los Angeles Times Sunday Magazine,* pp. 6, 12, 18.

Mitchel, M. (1936). *Gone with the wind.* New York: Macmillan.

Montville, L. (1987, February). [Feature article about Australia.] KNT News Service.

Morrow, L. (1987, February 23). Africa. *Time.*

Murrow, E. R. (1941). *This is London.* New York: Simon & Schuster.

Nack, W. (1987, January 19). I have to do right. *Sports Illustrated,* p. 73.

Newsweek. [Political obituary of James Watt.]

Orwell, G. (1949). *1984.* London: Secker and Warburg.

Payne, D. (1975). *The man of only yesterday: Frederick Lewis Allen.* New York: Harper & Row.

Phinney, K. (1988, April 1). Inventive ideas frittered away in *Beetlejuice. The Austin American Statesman,* p. C8.

Price, S. S. (1987, February 9). Quick—somebody get me rewrite. *The Daily Texan,* TV Watch sect., p. 2.

Randi, J. (1986, December 14). Not like the rest of us. *The New York Times Book Review,* p. 1.

Rosenberg, H. (1987, October). [Profile of Madlyn Rhue.] *The Los Angeles Times* News Service.

Rowan, R. (1986, November 10). The 50 biggest Mafia bosses. *Fortune,* pp. 24–32, 34, 36, 38.

Ryan, D. (1987, January 18). War as reality. *The Fort Worth Star Telegram,* p. D1.

Sacks, O. (1986). *The man who mistook his wife for a hat and other clinical tales.* New York: Summit Books.

Salinger, J. D. (1951). *The catcher in the rye.* Boston: Little, Brown.

Sanz, C. (1984, October 1). What stops hearts, is somewhat sadistic and is 100 years old? *The Wall Street Journal,* p. 1.

Schlesinger, J. M., & Guiles, M. G., (1987, January 16). Struggling back. *The Wall Street Journal,* p. 1.

Schleuse, D. L. The original Christmas store.

Sheed, W. (1986, December). Branch Rickey. *Sport,* pp. 29, 137.

Sheed, W. (1987). *The boys of winter.* New York: Knopf.

Schenkman, W. (1981, September–October). Vita: Johann Mattheson. *Harvard University Magazine,* p. 37.

Sloan, W. D., McCrary, C., & Cleary, J. (1986). *The best of Pulitzer Prize news writing.* Columbus, OH: Publishing Horizons.

Smith, W. W. (Red). (1951, October 26). Night for Joe Lewis. The New York *Herald Tribune.*

Stamberg, S. (1982). *Every night at five.* New York: Pantheon.

Steel, R. (1980). *Walter Lippmann and the American century.* Boston: Atlantic Monthly Press/Little, Brown.

Steinbeck, J. (1945). *Cannery Row.* New York: Viking Press.

Steinbeck, J. (1951). *The log from the Sea of Cortez.* New York: Viking Press.

Stengel, R. (1986, December 8). How Reagan stays out of touch. *Time,* p. 34.

Stoda, G. (1986, November 14). Busy picking cotton. *The Dallas Times Herald,* p. C1.

Streitfield, D. (1987, January). Excess on the rocks. *The Washington Post* News Service.

Taggart, P. ?1985, March 30). "King David" film just rolls over and plays dead. *The Austin American Statesman,* p. 44.

Taylor, R. B. (1987, January). [Feature article about cattle drives in the Sierra Nevada.] *The Los Angeles Times* News Service.

Uhlig, M. A. (1987, December 5). Open road beckons to adventurer, age 5. *The New York Times* News Service.

Vonnegut, K., Jr. (1963). *Cat's cradle.* New York: Holt, Rinehart & Winston.

Walsh, M. (1988, January 18). Magician of the musical. *Time,* p. 54.

Warren, R. P. (1946). *All the king's men.* New York: Harcourt, Brace.

Waters, H. F., & Goldberg, L. (1985, October 14). Small screen's big credits. *Newsweek,* p. 99.

Wiltse, D. (1986, March 9). Chopping down a forest of bad guys. *The New York Times Book Review,* p. 12.

Wysocki, A. M. (1983). Baseball, hotdogs, apple pie and folk art.

Name/Title Index

Subject Index